G000116148

Contents

Classic Swiss Cheese Fondue

Ingredients

- 1½ pounds Gruyère cheese

- 2 tablespoons cornstarch

- 1 loaf French bread

- 3 tablespoons kirsch

- 1 garlic clove

- 1/8 teaspoon cayenne pepper

- 1½ cups dry white wine

- 1 tablespoon lemon juice

- 1 tablespoon caraway seeds

Directions

1. Finely dice the Gruyère cheese and set aside. Cut the French bread into cubes and set aside.

2. Smash the garlic, peel, and cut in half. Rub the garlic around the inside of a medium saucepan. Discard. Add the wine to the saucepan and warm on medium-low heat. Don't allow the wine to boil.

3. When the wine is warm, stir in the lemon juice. Add the cheese, a handful at a time. Stir the cheese continually in a sideways figure eight pattern. Wait until the cheese is completely melted before adding more. Don't allow the fondue mixture to boil.

4. When the cheese is melted, dissolve the cornstarch in the kirsch and add to the cheese, stirring. Turn up the heat until it is just bubbling and starting to thicken. Stir in the cayenne pepper and caraway seeds. Transfer to a fondue pot and set on the burner. Serve with the French bread for dipping.

Neuchâtel Two Cheese Fondue

Ingredients

- ½ pound Emmenthal cheese

- 2 tablespoons kirsch

- ½ pound Gruyère cheese

- ¼ teaspoon nutmeg

- 1 garlic clove

- A pinch of black pepper

- 1 cup dry white wine

- 1 large parsley sprig, minced

- 2 teaspoons lemon juice

- Toasted Bread Cubes

- 1½ tablespoons cornstarch

Directions

1. Finely dice the cheeses and set aside. Smash the garlic and cut in half.

2. Rub the garlic around the inside of a medium saucepan. Discard. Add the wine to the pan and cook on low heat. Don't allow the wine to boil.

3. When the wine is warm, stir in the lemon juice. Add the cheese, a handful at a time. Stir the cheese continually in a sideways figure eight pattern. Wait until the cheese is completely melted before adding more. Don't allow the fondue mixture to boil.

4. When the cheese is melted, dissolve the cornstarch in the kirsch and stir into the cheese. Turn up the heat until it is just bubbling and starting to thicken. Stir in the nutmeg, black pepper, and parsley. Transfer to a fondue pot and set on the burner. Serve with the bread cubes for dipping.

Marinated Cheese Fondue

Ingredients

- 2 cups apple juice

- ¼ cup cornstarch

- 4 teaspoons lemon juice

- 6 tablespoons kirsch

- 2 servings Marinated Cheese Cubes

- 1 loaf French bread, cut into cubes

1. Warm the apple juice in a saucepan on medium-low heat. When the juice is warm, add the lemon juice. Add the cheese cubes a handful at a time, and stir continuously in a sideways figure eight pattern. Do not add more cheese until it is completely melted.

2. When all the cheese is melted, dissolve the cornstarch in the kirsch and stir into the cheese mixture. Turn up the heat until it just begins to bubble and thicken. Transfer to a fondue pot

and set on the burner. Serve with the French bread for dipping.

Swiss Cheese and Apple Fondue

Ingredients

- ½ pound Emmenthal cheese

- 1 cup Spicy Apple Chutney

- 1 baguette

- 1 garlic clove

- 2 teaspoons cornstarch

- 1 cup dry white wine

- 3 teaspoons water

1. Cut the cheese into thin slices and the baguette into cubes.

2. Smash the garlic, peel, and cut in half. Rub the inside of a medium saucepan with the garlic. Discard. Add the wine to the pan and cook on low heat. Don't allow the wine to boil.

3. When the wine is warm, stir in the chutney and heat through.

4. Dissolve the cornstarch in the water and stir into the fondue to thicken. As soon as the mixture thickens, transfer to a fondue pot and set on the burner. Serve with the sliced cheese for dipping. Eat the bread with the dipped cheese. If you run out of cheese, dip the bread into the fondue.

Plowman's Lunch Fondue

Ingredients

- 1 pound Gruyère cheese

- 1½ tablespoons water

- 1 garlic clove

- ¼ teaspoon ground white pepper, or to taste

- 2 tablespoons butter or margarine

- 1 teaspoon turmeric

- 1 cup dry white wine

- 1 loaf sun-dried tomato bread

- 2 teaspoons lemon juice

- 1 jar pickles

- 1 tablespoon cornstarch

Directions

1. Finely dice the Gruyère cheese and set aside. Smash the garlic, peel, and cut in half. Rub the garlic around the inside of a medium saucepan and discard. Add the butter and stir over low heat until it melts.

2. Add the wine. When the wine is warm, stir in the lemon juice. Add the cheese, a handful at a time. Stir the cheese continually in a sideways figure eight pattern. Wait until the cheese is completely melted before adding more. Don't allow the fondue mixture to boil.

3. When the cheese is completed melted, dissolve the cornstarch in the water and stir into the cheese. Turn up the heat until it is just bubbling and starting to thicken. Stir in the white pepper and turmeric. Transfer the fondue to a fondue pot and set on the burner. Slice the bread into cubes. Use dipping forks to dip the bread cubes into the cheese. Eat with the pickles.

Curry Fondue

Ingredients

- 2 fresh green jalapeño peppers

- 1 tablespoon cornstarch

- ¼ pound aged Cheddar cheese

- 1½ tablespoons kirsch

- ¼ pound Havarti with dill

- 1¼ teaspoons mild curry powderpowder powder

- ½ pound Gruyère cheese

- 1 garlic clove

- 12–15 grape tomatoes, sliced

- 1¼ cups white wine

- Basic Bruschetta (), cut into cubes
- 2 teaspoons lemon juice

Directions

1. Slice the jalapeño peppers lengthwise, remove the seeds, and chop coarsely. Dice the Cheddar and Havarti cheeses, and finely dice the Gruyère cheese. Smash the garlic, peel, and cut in half. Rub the garlic around the inside of a medium saucepan. Discard.

2. Add the wine to the pot and cook on low heat. Don't allow the wine to boil. When the wine is warm, stir in the lemon juice. Add the cheese, a handful at a time. Stir the cheese continually in a bowtie or sideways figure eight pattern. Wait until the cheese is completely melted before adding more. Don't allow the cheese to boil.

3. When the cheese is melted, dissolve the cornstarch in the kirsch and add to the cheese, stirring. Turn up the heat until it is just bubbling and starting to thicken. Add the chili peppers. Stir in the curry powder.

4. Transfer to a fondue pot and set on the burner. Serve with the bruschetta cubes and the grape tomatoes for dipping. (Use dipping forks to dip the grape tomatoes into the fondue).

Sweet Herb Fondue

Ingredients

- Sweet Herb Mix
- 1 garlic clove, smashed and cut in half
- 1½ cups dry white wine
- ½ pound Emmenthal cheese
- 1 teaspoon lemon juice
- ½ pound Havarti cheese with dill
- 3 teaspoons cornstarch
- 4 teaspoons water
- ¼ pound medium Cheddar cheese
- 1 sourdough baguette, cut into cubes

Directions

1. Add the Sweet Herb Mix to the wine and leave for 2 hours.

2. Finely dice the Emmenthal, and dice the Havarti and Cheddar cheeses. Smash the garlic clove, peel, and cut in half. Rub the garlic around the inside of a medium saucepan. Discard. Warm the wine-and-herb mixture on medium-low heat. Do not bring the wine to a boil.

3. When the wine is warm, add the lemon juice. Remove the bay leaf (which was contained in the Sweet Herb Mix) from the wine. Add the cheese, a handful at a time. Stir the cheese continually in a sideways figure eight pattern. Wait until the cheese is completely melted before adding more.

4. When the cheese is melted, dissolve the cornstarch in the water and add to the cheese, stirring. Turn up the heat until it is just bubbling and starting to thicken. Transfer to a fondue pot and set on the burner. Serve with the baguette cubes for dipping.

Blue Cheese Fondue

Ingredients

- 1 pound blue cheese
- 2 tablespoons flour
- 1 loaf French bread
- 1 cup milk
- 6 ounces cooked ham
- ¼ teaspoon nutmeg
- 2 tablespoons butter or margarine
- ¼ teaspoon paprika
- 1 tablespoon sour cream

Directions

1. Crumble the blue cheese and set aside. Cut the French bread into cubes and thinly slice the ham.

2. Melt the butter in a saucepan over medium-low heat and stir in the flour. Slowly add the milk, stirring.

3. Add the crumbled blue cheese, a handful at a time. Stir the cheese continually in a bowtie or

sideways figure eight pattern. Wait until the cheese is completely melted before adding more. Don't allow the cheese to boil.

4. When the cheese is melted, turn the heat up until it is just bubbling and starting to thicken. Stir in the nutmeg and paprika. Transfer to a fondue pot and set on the burner. Just before serving, swirl in the sour cream. Serve with the French bread cubes for dipping and eat with the ham slices.

Sweet Goat Cheese with Roasted Red Peppers

Ingredients

- 1½ pounds goat cheese

- 2 tablespoons chopped fresh tarragon

- 1 garlic clove

- 1½ cups dry white wine

- 1 loaf stale bread

- 1 tablespoon lemon juice

- ¼ cup olive oil

- 1 tablespoon cornstarch

- Roasted Red Peppers

- 3 tablespoons kirsch

Directions

1. Crumble the goat cheese. Smash the garlic, peel, and cut in half. Rub the garlic around the inside of a medium saucepan. Discard. Add the wine to the pan and warm on medium-low heat. Don't allow the wine to boil.

2. When the wine is warm, stir in the lemon juice. Add the cheese, a handful at a time, and stir continuously in a sideways figure eight pattern. Wait until the cheese is completely melted before adding more. Don't allow the fondue mixture to boil.

3. When the cheese is melted, dissolve the cornstarch in the kirsch and add to the cheese, stirring. Turn the heat up until it is just bubbling and starting to thicken. Stir in the fresh

tarragon leaves. Transfer to a fondue pot and set on the burner. Toast the bread and drizzle a small amount of olive oil around the edges. Cut into cubes. Serve the fondue with the peppers as a side dish and the stale bread for dipping

Fondue Provolone

Ingredients

- ½ pound provolone cheese

- 1 garlic clove

- 1 pound Emmenthal cheese

- 1½ cups dry white wine

- 2 tablespoons flour

- 2 tablespoons lemon juice

- ½ teaspoon dried basil, or to taste

- 2 tablespoons tomato paste

- 1 loaf French or Italian bread, cut into cubes

- ⅛ teaspoon dried oregano, or to taste

Directions

1. Finely dice the provolone and Emmenthal cheeses. Mix the flour with the basil and oregano. Toss the two cheeses with the flour and spices.

2. Smash the garlic, peel, and cut in half. Rub the garlic around the inside of a medium saucepan. Discard. Add the wine to the saucepan and warm on medium-low heat. Don't allow the wine to boil.

3. When the wine is warm, stir in the lemon juice. Add the cheese, a handful at a time. Stir the cheese continually in a sideways figure eight pattern. Wait until the cheese is completely melted before adding more. Don't allow the fondue mixture to boil.

4. When the cheese is melted, stir in the tomato paste. Heat through, and then turn up the heat until the mixture bubbles and starts thickening. Transfer to a fondue pot and set on the burner. Serve with the bread cubes for dipping.

Four Spice Cheese Fondue

Ingredients

- 1 pound spiced Gouda cheese
- 1 small bay leaf
- 1 tablespoon flour
- 1 cup Heineken beer
- $\frac{1}{8}$ teaspoon garlic salt
- 2 teaspoons lemon juice
- $\frac{1}{8}$ teaspoon black pepper
- 1½ teaspoons cornstarch
- ¼ cup red onion, finely chopped
- 1 teaspoon cognac
- 1½ tablespoons butter or margarine
- Toasted Bread Cubes 3 apples, sliced

Directions

1. Remove the rind from the Gouda cheese and shred.

2. Mix together the flour, garlic salt, and black pepper. Toss with the cheese.

3. Sauté the onion in the butter or margarine. Add the bay leaf and cook until the onion is soft and translucent. Remove the bay leaf.

4. Warm the beer in a medium saucepan but do not boil. When the beer is warm, add the lemon juice. Add the cheese gradually, stirring constantly in a sideways figure eight pattern. Wait until the cheese is completely melted before adding more. Don't allow the fondue mixture to boil.

5. When the cheese is nearly melted, add the onion. Stir for another minute; then dissolve the cornstarch in the cognac and stir into the fondue. Turn up the heat until the fondue is just bubbling and starting to thicken. Transfer to a fondue pot and set on the burner. Serve with the bread cubes and apples for dipping. (Broccoli, cauliflower, and mushrooms also make good dippers for this recipe.)

Pub Fondue

Ingredients

- 1¼ pounds medium Cheddar cheese

- 1 small shallot, chopped

- 1 cup beer, preferably flat

- 1 tablespoon flour

- 2 teaspoons lemon juice

- 1 sprig parsley, chopped

- 2 teaspoons Worcestershire sauce

- A pinch (no more than $\frac{1}{8}$ teaspoon) garlic powder

- 4 apples, cored and cut into thin slices

- 1 teaspoon paprika

- 1 tablespoon butter or margarine

- 1 sourdough baguette, cut into cubes

- ½ cup onion, chopped

Directions

1. Cut the Cheddar cheese into cubes. Combine the flour, parsley, garlic powder, and paprika. Toss the cubed cheese with the flour mixture and set aside.

2. Melt the butter or margarine in a pan. Add the onion and shallot and sauté until the onion is translucent but not browned. Turn off the heat and let sit in the pan.

3. Warm the beer in a medium saucepan, without bringing to a boil. Add the lemon juice. Add the cheese gradually, a handful at a time, stirring constantly. Make sure the cheese doesn't come to a boil. Don't add more until the cheese is fully melted.

4. When the cheese is nearly melted, add the onion and shallot. Stir for another minute, and then turn up the heat until it is just bubbling and starting to thicken. Stir in the Worcestershire sauce. Transfer to a fondue pot and set on the burner. Serve with the sliced apples and baguette cubes for dipping. Add other dippers such as pickles and tomatoes as desired.

Dieter's Fondue

Ingredients

- 2 ounces of any reduced-fat hard cheese
- $^1/_3$ cup cranberry juice
- 1 garlic clove
- ½ cup skim milk
- 4 tablespoons margarine
- 2 cups cottage cheese
- 4 tablespoons flour
- 2 tablespoons chopped fresh basil
- Black pepper to taste
- ¼ teaspoon cayenne pepper
- 2 parsley sprigs, chopped
- 1 package breadsticks

Directions

1. Dice the hard cheese. In a metal bowl, combine the skim milk, cottage cheese, basil, parsley, and cranberry juice.

2. Smash the garlic clove, peel, and cut in half. Rub garlic around the inside of a medium saucepan; discard. Add the margarine and melt on low heat. Stir in the flour.

3. Add the cottage cheese mixture and the hard cheese. Stir slowly over low heat until the cheese is melted and the mixture thickens. Stir in the black pepper and cayenne pepper. Whisk to remove any lumps in the flour if necessary.

4. Transfer the mixture to a fondue pot and set on the burner. Serve with the breadsticks for dipping.

Ham and Cheese Fondue

Ingredients

- 1¼ pounds medium Cheddar cheese

- 2 teaspoons lemon juice
- 1 tablespoon cornstarch
- 1 baguette
- 1½ tablespoons water
- 1 cup mushrooms
- 1 teaspoon kirsch
- 1½ cups cooked ham
- 2 teaspoons Worcestershire sauce
- 1 green onion
- 2 tablespoons butter or margarine
- ⅛ teaspoon black pepper, or to taste
- 1 cup beer

Directions

1. Cut the Cheddar cheese into cubes and set aside. Slice the baguette into cubes and set aside. Wipe the mushrooms with a damp cloth and slice. Cut the cooked ham into cubes. Dice the green onion.

2. Heat the butter in a medium saucepan. Add the mushrooms and sauté until tender. Add the beer and warm on low heat. When the beer is warm, add the lemon juice. Add the cheese gradually, stirring continually in a sideways figure eight pattern until it is completely melted.

3. When the cheese is melted, dissolve the cornstarch in the water and add to the cheese, stirring. Turn up the heat until it is just bubbling and starting to thicken. Add the kirsch, the Worcestershire sauce, and the black pepper. Taste and adjust the seasonings if desired.

4. Transfer the cheese to a fondue pot and set on the burner. Invite guests to place a baguette cube and a piece of ham on their fork before dipping into the fondue.

Tropical Fondue

Ingredients

- 2 mangoes

- 2 tablespoons kirsch

- ½ pound Emmenthal cheese

- ¼ teaspoon nutmeg

- ½ pound Gruyère cheese

- Black pepper to taste

- 1 garlic clove

- 1 cup Mint and Cilantro Chutney

- 1¾ cups dry white wine

- 2 teaspoons lemon juice

- Toasted Bread Cubes

- ½ tablespoon cornstarch

Directions

1. Cut the two mangoes in half, remove the pits, and cut into slices. Finely dice the cheeses.

2. Smash the garlic, peel, and cut in half. Rub the garlic around the inside of a medium saucepan. Discard. Add the wine to the pan and cook on low heat. Don't allow the wine to boil.

3. When the wine is warm, stir in the lemon juice. Add the cheese, a handful at a time. Stir the cheese continually in a sideways figure eight pattern. Wait until the cheese is completely melted before adding more. Don't allow the fondue mixture to boil.

4. When the cheese is melted, dissolve the cornstarch in the kirsch and stir into the cheese. Turn up the heat until it just bubbles and starts to thicken. Stir in the nutmeg and black pepper. Add the chutney. Thin the mixture by adding another ¼ cup of warmed wine if desired.

5. Transfer to a fondue pot and set on the burner. Serve with the bread cubes and sliced mangoes for dipping.

Breakfast Fondue

Ingredients

- 1 loaf bread

- 2 tablespoons Worcestershire sauce

- ¾ pound Gruyère cheese

- ¾ pound Emmenthal cheese

- Salt and pepper to taste

- 2 green onions

- 12 eggs

- 1 garlic clove

- 1 teaspoon cornstarch

- 1½ cups dry white wine

- 2 teaspoons water

- 1 tablespoon lemon juice

Directions

1. Toast the bread, cut into squares, and set aside. Finely dice the cheeses. Mince the green onions.

2. Smash the garlic, peel, and cut in half. Rub the garlic around the inside of a medium saucepan. Discard. Add the wine to the pan and warm on medium-low heat. Don't allow the wine to boil.

3. When the wine is warm, stir in the lemon juice. Add the cheese, a handful at a time. Stir the cheese continually in a sideways figure eight pattern. Wait until the cheese is completely melted before adding more. Don't allow the fondue mixture to boil.

4. When the cheese is melted, turn up the heat until it is just bubbling and starting to thicken. Stir in the Worcestershire sauce, salt and pepper, and green onion. Whisk in the eggs and scramble. Dissolve the cornstarch in the water and add to the mixture to thicken. Transfer to a fondue pot and set on the burner. Serve with the toasted bread for dipping.

Chèvre Fondue

Ingredients

- 1½ pounds chèvre goat cheese

- 1 tablespoon cornstarch

- 2 tablespoons fresh basil, chopped

- 3 tablespoons kirsch

- ¼ teaspoon paprika

- 1 tomato

- 1 loaf sourdough bread, cut into cubes

- ¼ cup margarine

- 1 garlic clove

- Marinated Tomatoes

- 1½ cups dry white wine, divided

Directions

1. Crumble the goat cheese and toss with the chopped basil. Wash the tomato, pat dry, and slice.

2. Heat the margarine in a frying pan and sauté the sliced tomato. Turn down the heat and keep warm while preparing the fondue.

3. Smash the garlic, peel, and cut in half. Rub the garlic around the inside of a saucepan. Leave the garlic in the pan and add 1¼ cups of wine. Warm the wine over medium-low heat but do not allow to boil.

4. When the wine is warm, add the goat cheese, a handful at a time. Stir the cheese continually in a sideways figure eight pattern. Wait until the cheese is completely melted before adding more. (Goat cheese melts quite quickly.) Don't allow the fondue mixture to come to a boil.

5. When the cheese is melted, dissolve the cornstarch in the kirsch and stir into the cheese mixture. Turn up the heat until it is just bubbling and starting to thicken. Stir in the paprika. Add the remaining ¼ cup of wine if necessary. Stir in the sliced tomato. Transfer to a fondue pot and set on the burner. Serve with the sourdough bread cubes for dipping. Eat with the Marinated Tomatoes.

Dutch Fondue

Ingredients

- 1 pound Gouda cheese

- 1½ cups Heineken Beer

- ½ pound Edam cheese

- 4 bay leaves

- 1½ tablespoons flour

- 1½ tablespoons kirsch

- 3 teaspoons caraway seeds

- ½ teaspoon nutmeg

- ½ teaspoon ground cumin

- 1 baguette, cut into cubes

Directions

1. Remove the rind from the Gouda cheese. Finely dice the Edam and the Gouda. Combine the flour, caraway seeds, and cumin. Toss the cheese with the flour mixture.

2. Place the beer in a medium saucepan and add the bay leaves. Warm the beer on low heat, being sure not to boil. When the beer is warm, remove the bay leaves.

3. Add the cheese gradually, stirring continually in a bowtie or sideways figure eight motion. Wait until the cheese has completely melted before adding more. Don't allow the fondue mixture to boil.

4. When the cheese is completely melted, turn up the heat until it just bubbles and starts to thicken. Stir in the kirsch and the nutmeg.

5. Transfer to a fondue pot and set on the burner. Serve with the baguette cubes for dipping.

Three Cheese Fondue

Ingredients

- 1 loaf stale bread

- 1 tablespoon lemon juice

- ½ pound Gruyère cheese

- 1 teaspoon cornstarch

- ½ pound Emmenthal cheese

- 2 tablespoons kirsch

- ½ pound Tilsit cheese

- Freshly ground white pepper to taste

- 1 garlic clove

- 1½ cups dry white wine

- 1 sprig parsley, chopped

Directions

1. Toast the bread and cut into cubes. Finely dice the Gruyère and Emmenthal cheeses. Dice the Tilsit cheese.

2. Smash the garlic, peel, and cut in half. Rub the garlic around the inside of a medium saucepan. Discard. Add the wine to the pan and warm on medium-low heat. Don't allow the wine to boil.

3. When the wine is warm, stir in the lemon juice. Add the cheese, a handful at a time. Stir the cheese continually in a sideways figure eight pattern. Wait until the cheese is completely melted before adding more. Don't allow the fondue mixture to boil.

4. When the cheese is completely melted, dissolve the cornstarch in the kirsch and stir into the fondue. Turn up the heat until it is just bubbling and starting to thicken. Stir in the white pepper and parsley. Transfer to a fondue pot and set on the burner. Serve with the toast cubes for dipping.

"Crab Rangoon" Fondue

Ingredients

- 2 pounds broccoli and cauliflower

- 8 ounces cream cheese

- 1 teaspoon Worcestershire sauce

- 1 tablespoon butter or margarine

- ½ teaspoon soy sauce

- ¼ cup onion, chopped

- ¼ cup milk

- 1 green onion

- 2 teaspoons lemon juice

- 6 ounces canned crabmeat, drained
- Crackers

Directions

1. Wash the broccoli and cauliflower and pat dry. Remove the stems and cut the flowerets into 1-inch pieces that can be speared with a dipping fork. Set aside.

2. Melt the butter or margarine in a frying pan. Sauté the onion until it is tender. Mince the green onion.

3. Combine the crabmeat, cream cheese, Worcestershire sauce, soy sauce, sautéed onion, and minced green onion. Mix thoroughly.

4. Rub the inside of a saucepan with a piece of onion. Warm the milk in the saucepan on medium-low heat. Add the lemon juice. Gradually add the crabmeat mixture, stirring.

5. Transfer to a fondue pot and set on the burner. Serve with the broccoli and cauliflower for dipping. Eat with the crackers.

Raspberry Swirl

Ingredients

- 1 pound Havarti cheese
- 2 teaspoons lemon juice
- 1½ cups fresh raspberries
- 4 teaspoons cornstarch
- 4 teaspoons lime juice
- 5 teaspoons water
- 4 teaspoons sugar
- 1 baguette, cut into cubes
- ¾ cup dry white wine, divided

Directions

1. Dice the Havarti cheese. Wash and drain the raspberries. Process the berries, lime juice, and sugar in a blender or food processor until smooth.

2. Warm ½ cup of the wine in a medium saucepan on medium-low heat. Don't allow the wine to

boil. Keep the remaining ¼ cup of wine warming in a separate saucepan.

3. When the wine is warm, stir in the lemon juice. Add the cheese, a handful at a time. Stir the cheese continually in a sideways figure eight pattern. Wait until the cheese is completely melted before adding more. Don't allow the fondue mixture to boil.

4. When the cheese is melted, stir in the raspberry purée and heat through. Dissolve the cornstarch in the water and add to the cheese, stirring. Turn up the heat until it is just bubbling and starting to thicken. Add the remaining ¼ cup of wine if necessary. Transfer to a fondue pot and set on the burner. Serve with the baguette cubes for dipping.

Garlic Fondue

Ingredients

- 1½ pounds Gruyère cheese

- 2 tablespoons kirsch

- 5 garlic cloves

- 1 tablespoon dry mustard

- 1½ cups dry white wine

- 1 sun-dried tomato baguette, cut into cubes

- 2 teaspoons lemon juice

- 1½ tablespoons cornstarch

Directions

1. Remove the rind from the Gruyère cheese and finely dice.

2. Smash and peel the garlic cloves. Cut one of the cloves in half. Take one half and rub around the inside of a medium saucepan.

3. Add the wine and the garlic cloves and cook on low heat. Don't allow the wine to boil.

4. When the wine is warm, stir in the lemon juice. Add the cheese, a handful at a time. Stir the cheese continually in a sideways figure eight pattern. Wait until the cheese is completely melted before adding more. Don't allow the fondue mixture to boil.

5. When the cheese is melted, dissolve the cornstarch in the kirsch and stir into the cheese. Turn up the heat until it just bubbles and starts to thicken. Stir in the dry mustard. Transfer to a

fondue pot and set on the burner. Remove the garlic cloves if desired. Serve with the baguette cubes for dipping.

Italian Cheese Fiesta

Ingredients

- 12 ounces provolone cheese
- 7 ounces Asiago cheese
- 7 ounces Gorgonzola cheese
- 1 garlic clove
- 1 tablespoon plus 2 teaspoons flour
- 1 cup dry white wine
- 1 tablespoon plus 1 teaspoon lemon juice
- ½ teaspoon dried oregano
- 1/8 teaspoon garlic powder
- Italian breadsticks, for dipping

Directions

1. Finely dice the provolone and Gorgonzola cheeses. Mix the flour with the oregano and garlic powder. Toss the two cheeses with the flour and spices. Crumble the Asiago cheese into the mixture.

2. Smash the garlic, peel, and cut in half. Rub the garlic around the inside of a medium saucepan. Discard. Add the wine to the saucepan and warm on medium-low heat. Don't allow the wine to boil.

3. When the wine is warm, stir in the lemon juice. Add the cheese, a handful at a time. Stir the cheese continually in a sideways figure eight pattern. Wait until the cheese is completely melted before adding more. Don't allow the fondue mixture to boil.

4. When the cheese is melted, turn up the heat until it is just bubbling and starting to thicken. Transfer to a fondue pot and set on the burner. Serve with the Italian breadsticks for dipping.

Four Cheese Fondue

Ingredients

- ½ pound Emmenthal cheese

- 3 tablespoons brandy

- ½ pound Gruyère cheese

- Black pepper to taste

- ½ pound Havarti cheese

- ¼ teaspoon nutmeg, or to taste

- ½ green or red bell pepper

- 1 garlic clove

- 2 ounces Cheddar cheese, grated

- 2 cups white wine

- 1 French baguette, cut into cubes

- 1 tablespoon lemon juice

- 2 tablespoons cornstarch

Directions

1. Finely dice the Emmenthal and Gruyère cheeses, and dice the Havarti. Wash the bell pepper, pat dry, and cut into cubes.

2. Smash the garlic, peel, and cut in half. Rub the garlic around the inside of a saucepan. Add the wine and heat over medium-low heat until warm. Do not allow the wine to boil.

3. Stir in the lemon juice. Add the cheese, a handful at a time, and stir continually in a sideways figure eight pattern. Do not add more cheese until it is melted.

4. When all the cheese is nearly melted, stir in the bell pepper cubes. Dissolve the cornstarch in the brandy and stir into the cheese. Turn up the heat until it just bubbles and starts to thicken. Add the black pepper and nutmeg. Sprinkle the grated Cheddar cheese on top. Transfer to a fondue pot and set on the burner. Serve with the baguette cubes for dipping.

Autumn Harvest Fondue

Ingredients

- ¾ pound Emmenthal cheese

- 1 tablespoon lemon juice

- ¾ pound Gruyère cheese

- 2 tablespoons cornstarch

- 2 cinnamon sticks

- 3 tablespoons apple schnapps

- 1 tablespoon coriander seeds

- ¼ teaspoon nutmeg

- 1 whole star anise (optional)

- 3 cups sliced apples

- 1¾ cups apple juice

- Toasted Flatbread

Directions

1. Finely dice the cheeses. Break the cinnamon sticks into several pieces. Place the cinnamon, the coriander seeds, and the star anise (if using) on a piece of cheesecloth about 6 inches by 6 inches. Use a piece of string to tie the cheesecloth and attach a cork to the other end of the string.

2. Heat the apple juice in a saucepan over medium-low heat. When the apple juice is warm, stir in the lemon juice. Add the spice bag, keeping the cork over the side of the saucepan so the bag can be pulled out.

3. When the apple juice is warm, remove the spice bag. Add the cheese, a handful at a time, stirring continually in a sideways figure eight pattern. Do not add more cheese until it is melted.

4. When all the cheese is melted, dissolve the cornstarch in the apple schnapps and stir into the fondue. Turn up the heat until it just bubbles and starts to thicken. Stir in the nutmeg. Transfer to a fondue pot and set on the burner. Serve with the sliced apples and flatbread for dipping.

Swiss Appenzeller Fondue

Ingredients

- ½ pound Appenzeller cheese

- 2 tablespoons cognac

- ½ pound Gruyère cheese

- 1 teaspoon dry mustard

- ½ pound Emmenthal cheese

- Freshly ground black pepper to taste

- 1 garlic clove

- 1½ cups apple cider, divided

- 1 loaf stale bread, cut into cubes

- 2 teaspoons lemon juice

- 1 tablespoon cornstarch

Directions

1. Finely dice the cheeses and set aside.

2. Smash the garlic, peel, and cut in half. Rub the garlic around the inside of a medium saucepan. Discard. Add 1¼ cups apple cider to the saucepan and warm on medium-low heat, without allowing to boil.

3. When the cider is warm, stir in the lemon juice. Add the cheese, a handful at a time. Stir the cheese continually in a sideways figure eight pattern. Wait until the cheese is completely melted before adding more. Don't allow the fondue mixture to boil.

4. When the cheese is melted, dissolve the cornstarch in the cognac and add to the cheese, stirring. Turn up the heat until it is just bubbling and starting to thicken. If necessary, add the remaining ¼ cup of cider. Stir in the dry mustard and freshly ground pepper. Transfer to a fondue pot and set on the burner. Serve with the bread cubes for dipping.

Italian Cheese Fondue with Béchamel Sauce

Ingredients

- ¾ pound Gorgonzola cheese

- 1 tablespoon cornstarch

- ¾ pound mozzarella cheese

- 2 tablespoons cream

- 1 clove garlic

- 1 teaspoon nutmeg

- 1¼ cups milk, divided

- 2 tablespoons brandy

- 2 tablespoons butter

- 1 loaf Italian bread, cut into cubes

- 2 tablespoons flour

Directions

1. Finely dice the Gorgonzola and mozzarella. Smash the garlic, peel, and cut in half.

2. Warm the milk in a small saucepan. In a separate medium saucepan, rub the garlic around the inside and then discard the garlic. Melt the butter in the saucepan with the garlic and stir in the flour. Add 1 cup of the warmed milk. Cook over low heat for about 10 minutes, whisking to form a creamy sauce.

3. Add the cheese, a handful at a time. Stir the cheese continually in a sideways figure eight pattern. Wait until the cheese is completely melted before adding more. Don't allow the fondue mixture to boil. Add the remaining ¼ cup of milk as needed.

4. When the cheese is melted, dissolve the cornstarch in the cream and add to the fondue, stirring. Turn up the heat until it is just bubbling and starting to thicken. Stir in the nutmeg and the brandy. Transfer to a fondue pot and set on the burner. Serve with the Italian bread cubes for dipping.

Ricotta Cheese in Apple Cider

Ingredients

- ½ loaf whole wheat bread, sliced

- 2 teaspoons lemon juice

- 1 garlic clove

- 1 pound ricotta cheese

- 1 cup apple cider

- 2 teaspoons caraway seeds

Directions

1. Toast the bread slices and cut into cubes approximately 1 inch thick.

2. Smash the garlic, peel, and cut in half. Rub the garlic around the inside of a medium saucepan. Discard. Add the apple cider to the saucepan and warm on medium-low heat.

3. When the cider is warmed, stir in the lemon juice. Gradually stir in the cheese. Stir the cheese continually in a sideways figure eight pattern to soften. When the cheese has melted, turn up the heat until it is just bubbling and starting to thicken. Stir in the caraway seeds. Transfer to a fondue pot and set on the burner. Serve with the toasted bread cubes for dipping.

Deep-Fried Cheese

Ingredients

- ½ pound Cheddar cheese

- ½ teaspoon sugar

- ½ pound Monterey Jack cheese

- 3 cups oil, or as needed

- 2 eggs

- ½ cup flour

- 1 tablespoon milk

- Quick and Easy Batter

- ¼ teaspoon paprika

Directions

1. Cut the cheeses into cubes, about ¾ inch thick. Beat the eggs with the milk, paprika, and sugar. Make sure the eggs are beaten thoroughly.

2. Add the oil to the fondue pot, making sure it is not more than half full. Heat the pot on a stove element over medium-high heat.

3. When the oil is hot, move the fondue pot to the table and set up the burner. Coat the cheese cubes with the flour. Dip the cheese into the egg wash and then cover with the batter. Spear

the cheese with a dipping fork and cook in the hot oil until the batter browns (about 30 to 40 seconds). Drain on paper towels if desired. Cool and eat.

Parmigiano-Reggiano Classic

Ingredients

- 1 fresh truffle

- 1 garlic clove

- 4 ounces Parmigiano-Reggiano cheese

- 1 cup dry white wine

- 1 tablespoon lemon juice

- 6 ounces Gorgonzola cheese

- 2 tablespoons cooked ham, chopped

- 1 tablespoon flour

- 1 tablespoon dried oregano

- Bruschetta Fondue Cubes with Vegetables

- 4 ounces Asiago cheese

Directions

1. Pat the truffle dry with a damp cloth and slice thinly. Remove the rinds from the Parmigiano-Reggiano and Gorgonzola cheeses and finely dice. Mix the flour with the oregano. Toss the two cheeses with the seasoned flour. Crumble the Asiago cheese into the mixture.

2. Smash the garlic, peel, and cut in half. Rub the garlic around the inside of a medium saucepan. Discard. Add the wine to the saucepan and warm on medium-low heat. Don't allow the wine to boil.

3. When the wine is warm, stir in the lemon juice. Add the cheese, a handful at a time. Stir the cheese continually in a sideways figure eight pattern. Wait until the cheese is completely melted before adding more. Don't allow the fondue mixture to boil.

4. When the cheese is melted, turn up the heat until it is just bubbling and starting to thicken. Transfer to a fondue pot and set on the burner. Just before serving, sprinkle with the chopped ham and sliced truffle. Serve with the bruschetta cubes for dipping.

Brie and Pesto

Ingredients

- 1 pound Brie cheese

- 2 teaspoons lemon juice

- 2 tablespoons flour

- Roasted Red Pepper Pesto

- 1 garlic clove

- 1 cup dry white wine

Directions

1. Cut the Brie into cubes. Toss the cheese cubes with the flour and set aside.

2. Smash the garlic, peel, and cut in half. Rub the garlic around the inside of a medium saucepan. Discard. Add the wine to the saucepan and warm on medium-low heat. Don't allow the wine to boil.

3. When the wine is warm, stir in the lemon juice. Add the cheese, a handful at a time. Stir the cheese continually in a sideways figure eight pattern. Wait until the cheese is completely melted before adding more. Don't allow the fondue mixture to boil.

4. When the cheese is melted, turn up the heat until it is just bubbling and starting to thicken. Stir in the Roasted Red Pepper Pesto. Heat through, transfer to a fondue pot, and set on the burner.

Curried Yogurt

Ingredients

- 1 cup plain yogurt

- ¾ teaspoon curry powder

- 1 teaspoon lemon juice

- 1 tablespoon water

- 1 teaspoon lime juice

- 1½ teaspoons garlic, chopped

Directions

1. Combine all the ingredients and process in a food processor or blender. Cover and refrigerate until ready to serve.

Seafood Cocktail Sauce

Ingredients

- ½ celery stalk
- ½ teaspoon Worcestershire sauce
- 3 teaspoons prepared horse-radish
- **Ingredients**
- ½ teaspoon hot chili sauce, or to taste
- 1 cup ketchup
- 2 teaspoons lemon juice
- ¼ teaspoon black pepper

Directions

1. Finely dice the celery until you have 4 tablespoons. Stir the horseradish into the ketchup. Add the diced celery. Combine the lemon juice with the Worcestershire sauce and add to the ketchup mixture. Stir in the chili sauce and black pepper.

2. For best results, cover and refrigerate for several hours before serving.

Sweet Herb Mix

Ingredients

- 1 sprig parsley, stem removed
- ⅓ bay leaf
- 1 sprig thyme
- A pinch (under ⅛ teaspoon) sage
- 1 mint leaf

Directions

1. Chop the parsley and thyme sprigs and shred the mint leaf. Combine all the ingredients together. Use immediately.

Sweet Banana Chutney

Ingredients

- 2 large bananas
- ¼ teaspoon allspice
- ⅓ cup balsamic vinegar
- 1 teaspoon water
- 1 teaspoon brown sugar

Directions

1. Peel and thinly slice the bananas. In a medium saucepan, bring the balsamic vinegar and sliced bananas to a boil. Continue to cook the mixture, stirring frequently, until the bananas and vinegar are fully blended. If using smaller bananas, add more slices as required.

2. Stir in the brown sugar and allspice. Add the water if needed. Heat through. Store in the refrigerator until ready to serve with the fondue.

Mint and Cilantro Chutney

Ingredients

- ⅓ cup cilantro leaves, chopped
- 1 teaspoon sugar
- ½ cup mint leaves, chopped
- 1 tablespoon dark raisins
- 3 tablespoons plain yogurt
- ⅛ teaspoon cayenne pepper, or to taste
- 1½ teaspoons lemon juice
- 1 tablespoon red onion, chopped

Directions

1. Combine all the ingredients and process in a blender or food processor until smooth.

Aioli

Ingredients

- 4 large garlic cloves

- ¾ cup extra-virgin olive oil

- 2 teaspoons lemon juice, or to taste

- Salt and freshly ground black pepper to taste

- 2 egg yolks

- Cayenne pepper to taste

Directions

1. Smash the garlic cloves, peel, and mash thoroughly with a mortar and pestle. Stir in the lemon juice. Stir in the egg yolks.

2. Add the olive oil, a few drops at a time, whisking constantly. After adding 2 to 3 teaspoons, the sauce should begin to take on the consistency of mayonnaise. Then you can begin adding the rest of the olive oil in a slow, steady stream, still whisking constantly.

3. Add the salt, pepper, and cayenne. Taste and adjust the seasonings if desired. Cover and refrigerate until ready to serve.

Quick and Easy Blender Hollandaise Sauce

Ingredients

- 2 tablespoons white wine vinegar

- ½ cup butter

- 2 tablespoons lemon juice

- 3 large egg yolks

- 2 tablespoons fresh dill, chopped

- ⅛ teaspoon cayenne pepper

Directions

1. Warm the white wine vinegar, lemon juice, and chopped dill. In a separate small saucepan, melt the butter and keep it hot without burning.

2. Place the white wine vinegar mixture in a blender and process for about 10 seconds. Add the egg yolks and the cayenne pepper.

3. Pour the butter into the blender and process on high speed for at least 40 seconds or until the sauce has thickened. (Note: If the sauce is not thick enough, place it in the top of a double boiler over hot, but not boiling, water, and whisk until thickened. Remove from the heat as soon as it's thickened.) Refrigerate until ready to serve.

Light Horseradish Dressing

Ingredients

- 2 sprigs parsley
- 2 tablespoons horseradish
- ⅔ cup plain yogurt
- 2 teaspoons lemon juice

Directions

1. Chop the parsley. Combine all the ingredients and serve the dressing immediately.

Marvelous Mango Chutney

Ingredients

- 1¼ cups mango flesh from 2 medium ripe mangoes
- 1 tablespoon sugar
- ¼ teaspoon salt
- ¼ cup balsamic vinegar
- A pinch (up to ⅛ teaspoon) chili powder, optional
- 3 tablespoons seedless raisins
- 1 teaspoon ginger, minced

Directions

1. To cut the mango flesh, cut a small slice off the stem end of the mango. Cut the mango in half, going around the pit in the middle. This will give you three sections: the section of flesh around the pit, and the two halves on either side. Cut the fruit around the section with the pit into small pieces. For the other two sections, lightly score the flesh without cutting through the skin, then gently push on the skin so it is almost turned inside out. The pieces of scored fruit will come out easily.

2. Combine the mango, balsamic vinegar, raisins, ginger, sugar, and salt in a saucepan and bring to a boil, stirring continually. Turn down the heat to low and let the chutney simmer, uncovered, for another 35–45 minutes.

3. If using the chili powder, add it at this point and simmer for another couple of minutes. Taste and adjust the seasonings as desired. Cool and refrigerate in a sealed container.

Honey Mustard Sauce

Ingredients

- ⅔ cup beef broth

- 3 tablespoons honey

- 3 tablespoons butter or margarine

- 1 teaspoon water

- ¼ teaspoon chili powder, or to taste

- 3 tablespoons flour

- 3 tablespoons Dijon mustard

Directions

If using homemade or packaged beef broth, warm the broth in a small saucepan. If using an instant bouillon cube, prepare according to the Directions on the package.

1. Combine the butter and flour in a saucepan over low heat, stirring. Slowly stir in ⅓ cup of the beef broth. Mix in the mustard and honey.

2. Add the remaining ⅓ cup of the beef broth. Turn up the heat to thicken. Add the water and the chili powder. Serve warm.

"Horseradish"

Ingredients

- ½ cup mayonnaise

- 4 teaspoons sugar

- 2 teaspoons garlic powder

- 1 teaspoon cayenne pepper, or to taste

- 2 teaspoons lemon juice

- 1 teaspoon chili powder

Directions

1. Combine all the ingredients. Serve immediately or store in a sealed container in the refrigerator.

Spicy Apple Chutney

Ingredients

- 2 apples, peeled, cored, and sliced

- 3 tablespoons sultana raisins

- 1 tablespoon plus 1 teaspoon sugar

- ½ cup rice vinegar

- ¼ teaspoon nutmeg

- ¼ teaspoon curry paste

- ¼ teaspoon cumin

- 2 tablespoons water

- 1 teaspoon lemon juice

Directions

1. Combine the apples, rice vinegar, nutmeg, cumin, lemon juice, raisins, sugar, and curry paste in a medium-sized saucepan. Bring to a boil, stirring continuously. Simmer for about 50 minutes, stirring occasionally, until the raisins are soft and the chutney has a texture similar to porridge. Add the 2 tablespoons of water if necessary.

2. Remove the chutney and process in a blender or food processor for just a few seconds so that it is well combined but chunky, not smooth. Refrigerate until ready to use.

Mild Curry Sauce

Ingredients

- ½ cup red onion, finely chopped

- 4 tablespoons flour

- 2 tablespoons plus 2 teaspoons garlic, finely chopped

- ½ cup plus 4 teaspoons unsweetened coconut flakes

- 1 teaspoon mild curry powder

- 2 tablespoons plus 2 teaspoons fresh ginger, finely chopped

- 1 cup chicken broth

- Cayenne pepper to taste

- Salt to taste

- ½ cup plus 4 teaspoons butter or margarine

Directions

1. Slowly cook the red onion, garlic, and ginger with the butter until the onion is tender. Stir in the flour. Add the coconut and the curry powder.

2. Add the chicken broth and turn up the heat to medium, stirring all the while to thicken. Add the cayenne pepper and salt. Mix well and serve warm.

Béarnaise Sauce

Ingredients

- $1/3$ cup white wine vinegar

- 1¼ tablespoons parsley, chopped

- 5 tablespoons white wine

- 1 tablespoon shallot, chopped

- ¼ teaspoon cayenne, or to taste

- 2½ tablespoons fresh tarragon, chopped

- Salt to taste

- $2/3$ cup butter

- ½ teaspoon sugar

- 4 large egg yolks

Directions

1. Combine the white wine vinegar, wine, shallot, and tarragon in a saucepan. Heat until the sauce is reduced to $1/3$ cup. Cool and strain by lining a funnel with cheesecloth, and then straining the sauce through the funnel.

2. While the white wine vinegar mixture is heating, melt the butter in a small saucepan. Keep the butter warm on low heat without burning.

3. Place the white wine vinegar mixture in the top of a double boiler, over water that is hot but not boiling. (If you don't have a double boiler, use a metal bowl placed over a saucepan half-filled with simmering water.) Make sure the bottom of the top boiler does not touch the heated water. Slowly add the egg yolks and butter, whisking constantly. When the mixture has thickened, whisk in the parsley, cayenne, salt, and sugar. Whisk until the sauce has thickened.

4. Serve the sauce immediately or cover and refrigerate until ready to serve. If preparing ahead of time, the refrigerated sauce can be served warm or cold. If serving warm, reheat by placing the bowl containing the sauce inside another bowl filled with hot water. Stir briefly. This prevents the sauce from curdling.

Homemade Tartar Sauce

Ingredients

- 2 egg yolks

- A pinch of cayenne

- ½ cup salad oil, divided

- 1 teaspoon capers (about 8), finely chopped

- ¼ teaspoon salt

- 1 tablespoon white wine vinegar

- 2 tablespoons onion, finely chopped

- 1 teaspoon lemon juice

- 1 pickle, chopped

- 1 teaspoon prepared mustard (such as Dijon)

Directions

1. Put the egg yolks into a metal bowl and whisk vigorously. Add 1 tablespoon salad oil and continue whisking. Repeat with a second tablespoon of salad oil. Whisk in the salt.

2. Add the white wine vinegar. Add 2 more tablespoons salad oil, a few drops at a time,

whisking vigorously. The mixture should emulsify and thicken.

3. Once the mixture has emulsified, add the lemon juice, mustard, cayenne, capers, onion, and pickle. Add the remaining ¼ cup of salad oil and process in a blender or food processor. For best results, chill for an hour to give the flavors a chance to blend.

Thai Peanut Sauce

Ingredients

- ½ cup peanut butter

- ½ cup plus 2 tablespoons coconut milk

- 4 tablespoons sugar

- 4 teaspoons red curry paste

- 1 teaspoon nuoc mam fish sauce

- 3 tablespoons plus 1 teaspoon lime juice

-

1. Combine all the ingredients except for the fish sauce in a blender or food processor. Process until smooth. Remove and add to a saucepan. Cook on low heat, stirring continuously, for at least 5 minutes. Stir in the fish sauce. Serve warm or at room temperature.

Basic Chinese Hot Mustard

Ingredients

- ½ cup dry mustard

- ½ cup water

Directions

1. Combine the dry mustard with the cold water to form a paste. The mustard will be at its hottest in 10–15 minutes, and will slowly weaken after that. For best results, use immediately.

Lemony Horseradish

Ingredients

- ½ cup mayonnaise

- 2 teaspoons shallot, finely chopped

- 4 teaspoons prepared horse-radish

- **Ingredients**

- 4 teaspoons lemon juice

- 1 teaspoon garlic powder

Directions

1. Combine the mayonnaise, horseradish, garlic powder, and shallot. For a stronger flavor, squeeze the excess vinegar out of the prepared horseradish. Stir in the lemon juice. Prepare just before serving and use immediately.

Quick and Easy Tartar Sauce

Ingredients

- 2 teaspoons capers (about 16), finely chopped

- 1 teaspoon parsley, chopped

- 2 tablespoons pickle, chopped

- ½ cup mayonnaise

- 2 teaspoons lemon juice

- 2 teaspoons onion, finely chopped

Directions

1. Rinse the capers. Combine all the ingredients except for the lemon juice and blend well. Stir in the lemon juice. For best results, refrigerate for at least 1 hour before serving to allow the flavors to blend.

Guacamole

Ingredients

- 2 avocados

- ½ teaspoon chili powder, or to taste

- ½ tomato

- 1½ green onions

- ¼ teaspoon ground cumin

- 4 teaspoons lemon juice

- 1 tablespoon mild salsa

Directions

1. Peel the avocados and slice lengthwise. Remove the pit and mash the flesh (a mortar and pestle is ideal for this). Chop the tomato into small pieces. Finely dice the green onions.

2. Mix the tomato and green onion with the mashed avocado. Stir in the lemon juice, chili powder, cumin, and salsa. For best results, refrigerate for 30 minutes to allow the flavors to blend, then serve.

Teriyaki-Style Dipping Sauce

Ingredients

- 1 green onion
- 1½ teaspoons brown sugar
- ⅓ cup lite soy sauce
- ⅛ teaspoon garlic powder
- ¼ cup pineapple juice
- A few drops Asian sesame oil

Directions

1. Dice the green onion. Combine the green onion with the soy sauce, pineapple juice, brown sugar, and garlic powder. Drizzle the sesame oil over and blend well. For best results, refrigerate the sauce until ready to use. Serve cold.

Soy and Wasabi Sauce

Ingredients

- 1 shallot
- 2 tablespoons butter
- 1 green onion
- 2 tablespoons lemon juice
- 1 tablespoon wasabi paste
- 1 teaspoon Dijon mustard, optional
- 6 tablespoons soy sauce, divided

Directions

1. Peel and chop the shallot. Mince the green onion. Mix the wasabi paste with 2 tablespoons of soy sauce and set aside.

2. In a small saucepan, melt the butter. Add the shallot and green onion and cook on low heat until the shallot is tender. Add the remaining 4 tablespoons of the soy sauce and the lemon juice.

3. Add the wasabi and soy sauce mixture. Stir in the Dijon mustard, if using. Keep stirring until the ingredients are blended together. Serve warm, immediately.

Horseradish with Sour Cream

Ingredients

- ½ cup sour cream
- ½ teaspoon ginger, minced
- 2 teaspoons shallots, minced
- 2 tablespoons prepared horse-radish

Directions

1. Combine all the ingredients. Cover and refrigerate until ready to use.

Horseradish Cream

Ingredients

- ½ cup whipping cream
- ½ teaspoon lemon juice
- 2 tablespoons prepared horseradish
- 1 teaspoon Worcestershire sauce

Directions

1. In a metal bowl, beat the whipping cream until it stiffens. Stir in the horseradish, lemon juice, and Worcestershire sauce. Cover and refrigerate until ready to serve.

Quick Honey Mustard

Ingredients

- ½ cup Dijon mustard
- Freshly ground white pepper to taste

- 2½ teaspoons honey

Directions

1. Blend all the ingredients together until smooth. Refrigerate for a few hours before serving to give the flavors time to blend.

Italian Pesto with Basil and Pine Nuts

Ingredients

- 1 cup packed fresh basil leaves

- 6 tablespoons extra-virgin olive oil

- 4 garlic cloves

- 4 tablespoons Parmesan cheese, grated

- 4 tablespoons pine nuts

Directions

1. Chop the basil leaves. Smash, peel, and chop the garlic. Process the basil, garlic, and pine nuts in a food processor or blender. Slowly add the olive oil and keep processing until the pesto is creamy. Add the grated Parmesan cheese. Serve immediately.

Roasted Red Pepper Pesto

Ingredients

- 2 Roasted Red Peppers

- 4 tablespoons Parmesan cheese, grated

- 4 garlic cloves

- 5 tablespoons olive oil

- 1½ cups packed parsley leaves

- Fresh cracked black pepper to taste

- 4 tablespoons pine nuts

Directions

1. Remove the skin from the roasted red peppers. Remove the seeds and chop the pepper finely. Smash and peel the garlic cloves.

2. Purée the roasted red peppers in a blender or food processor. Remove. Combine the parsley leaves, garlic cloves, and pine nuts in the food processor and chop. Mix the parsley mixture

with the puréed red peppers, and stir in the grated Parmesan cheese and olive oil. Add the fresh cracked black pepper. Serve immediately.

Cilantro and Mint Dressing

Ingredients

- 4 garlic cloves
- 2 tablespoons walnut pieces, chopped
- 1 fresh green jalapeño pepper
- $\frac{1}{3}$ cup packed cilantro leaves, chopped
- 2 teaspoons lemon juice
- 2 tablespoons Parmesan cheese, grated
- $\frac{1}{3}$ cup packed mint leaves, chopped
- 3 tablespoons olive oil
- 2 tablespoons pine nuts

Directions

1. Smash, peel, and mince the garlic cloves. Cut the jalapeño pepper lengthwise, remove the seeds, and chop coarsely.

2. Process the cilantro leaves, mint leaves, garlic, jalapeño pepper, pine nuts, walnut pieces, and lemon juice in a blender or food processor. Add the grated cheese and process again. Remove, place in a bowl, and slowly stir in the olive oil. Cover and refrigerate until ready to serve.

Pesto Mayonnaise

Ingredients

- Italian Pesto with Basil and Pine Nuts
- ½ teaspoon lemon juice
- 1 tablespoon plus 2 teaspoons mayonnaise

Directions

1. Place the pesto in a mixing bowl and stir in the mayonnaise and lemon juice. For best results, cover and refrigerate for 1 hour to give the flavors a chance to blend. Keep refrigerated until ready to use.

Golden Hot Mustard

Ingredients

- 2 teaspoons cold water
- 1 teaspoon sugar
- ¼ cup dry mustard
- 1 teaspoon turmeric
- 2 tablespoons vinegar

Directions

1. Cover and store in the refrigerator until ready to use.

Yogurt and Dill Dressing

Ingredients

- 1 cup yogurt
- 1 sprig fresh thyme leaves, stem removed
- 1 tablespoon plus 1 teaspoon lemon juice
- **Ingredients**
- 1½ teaspoons Dijon mustard, or to taste
- 1 tablespoon fresh baby dill, chopped

Directions

1. Combine all the ingredients. Refrigerate, covered, until ready to serve.

White Sauce for Seafood

Ingredients

- 2½ tablespoons butter
- 2 teaspoons lemon juice
- 2 tablespoons flour
- 1 parsley sprig, chopped
- 2 tablespoons cream
- Salt and pepper to taste

- 1 cup milk
- 4 capers, optional

Directions

1. Melt the butter in a saucepan on low heat. Blend in the flour thoroughly and cook for another 2 to 3 minutes, taking care not to burn the flour. Turn up the heat to medium-low and mix in the cream. Slowly add the milk, whisking constantly until the sauce thickens.

2. Stir in the lemon juice, parsley, and salt and pepper. Add capers, if using. Use immediately or keep warm on low heat, stirring occasionally, until ready to serve with the fondue.

White Sauce for Vegetables

Ingredients

- 2½ tablespoons butter, unsalted
- 1 cup milk
- 2 tablespoons flour
- ⅛ teaspoon celery salt
- 2 tablespoons cream
- ⅛ teaspoon paprika

Directions

1. Melt the butter in a saucepan on low heat. Blend in the flour thoroughly and cook for another 2 to 3 minutes, taking care not to burn the flour. Turn up the heat to medium-low and mix in the cream.

2. Slowly add the milk, whisking constantly until the sauce thickens and bubbles. Stir in the celery salt and paprika. Use immediately or keep warm on low heat, stirring occasionally, until ready to serve.

Speedy Garlic Mayonnaise

Ingredients

- 4 large garlic cloves
- 2 teaspoons Dijon mustard
- ¾ cup mayonnaise

Directions

1. Smash and peel the garlic. Using a mortar and pestle, mash the garlic thoroughly. In a bowl, mix the mashed garlic with the mayonnaise and Dijon mustard. Refrigerate until ready to serve.

Sour Cream and Mustard Dip

Ingredients

- ½ green onion

- 1 teaspoon lemon juice

- 1 cup sour cream

- 1 teaspoon fresh parsley, chopped

- 2½ tablespoons Dijon mustard

Directions

1. Mince the green onion. Combine all the ingredients. Refrigerate, covered, until ready to serve.

French Pistou with Cheese

Ingredients

- 1½ cups packed fresh basil leaves, chopped

- 4 tablespoons extra-virgin olive oil

- 3 or 4 large garlic cloves

- Freshly ground black pepper to taste

- 2 tablespoons Gruyère cheese, grated

Directions

1. Chop the basil leaves. Smash, peel, and chop the garlic cloves. Process the chopped basil, garlic, and grated Gruyère cheese in a food processor or blender. Slowly add the olive oil while continuing to process, until the pesto is a creamy paste. Season with the pepper.

Sukiyaki Sauce

Ingredients

- ½ cup soy sauce

- 2 tablespoons sugar

- ½ cup Vegetable Broth

- ¼ cup Japanese sake

Directions

1. Combine all the ingredients. Bring to a boil and let simmer for a few minutes before using.

Fondue Béchamel Sauce

Ingredients

- ¾ cup milk

- ½ cup total of Cheddar and Monterey Jack cheese, shredded

- 2 tablespoons butter

- 2 tablespoons flour

- 2 tablespoons cream

- 1 teaspoon caraway seeds

Directions

1. Warm the milk in a small saucepan. In a separate saucepan, melt the butter on low heat and stir in the flour. Be careful not to let the flour burn.

2. Add the cream to the butter-and-flour mixture. Blend well, and then slowly pour into the warmed milk. Cook over low heat for about 10 minutes, whisking continuously to form a creamy sauce.

3. Add the cheese, a handful at a time. Stir the cheese continually in a sideways figure eight pattern. Wait until the cheese is completely melted before adding more. Don't allow the fondue mixture to boil. Stir in the caraway seeds. Use immediately.

Extra Hot Pot Dipping Sauce

Ingredients

- 2 teaspoons coriander seeds

- ½ cup water

- ½ cup soy sauce

- 2 teaspoons hot chili sauce

- ½ cup peanut butter

- 2 tablespoons plus 2 teaspoons sugar

Directions

1. Grind the coriander seeds in a coffee grinder or with a mortar and pestle. Combine with the soy sauce, peanut butter, sugar, and water in a food processor or blender and process until smooth. Stir in the chili sauce. Store in a sealed container in the refrigerator until ready to use.

Hot Pot Dip for Beef

Ingredients

- 1 garlic clove

- ¼ cup water

- ¾ cup peanut butter

- 1 teaspoon hot chili sauce, or to taste

- ¼ cup chicken broth

- ½ cup dark soy sauce

- 1 teaspoon sesame seed oil, or to taste

- 4 teaspoons sugar

Directions

1. Smash, peel, and chop the garlic clove. Combine the chopped garlic, peanut butter, chicken broth, dark soy sauce, sugar, and water in a blender or food processor and process until smooth. Stir in the hot chili sauce and sesame seed oil and mix well. Store in a sealed container in the refrigerator until ready to use.

Lemon-Soy Dressing (Ponzu)

Ingredients

- 1 Chinese dried mushroom, optional

- ⅓ cup lemon juice

- ½ teaspoon rice vinegar

- ⅔ cup soy sauce

Directions

1. If using the dried mushroom, soak in warm water for 20 minutes to soften. Squeeze out the excess water and slice.

2. Combine all the ingredients. For best results, prepare a few hours ahead of time to give the flavors a chance to blend. Remove the dried mushroom slices before serving. The sauce will last for several days if stored in a sealed container in the refrigerator.

Sesame Dipping Paste

Ingredients

- 4 tablespoons plus 2 tea-spoons soybean paste

- 1 teaspoon rice vinegar

- 2 teaspoons sesame seeds

- 4 tablespoons chicken broth

- ½ teaspoon lemon juice

- 2 teaspoons soy sauce

Directions

1. Combine all the ingredients. For best results, make this strong flavored dip a few hours ahead of time to give the flavors a chance to blend.

Nut-Free Hot Pot Dipping Sauce

Ingredients

- ¼ cup soy sauce

- 1 tablespoon plus 1 teaspoon sugar

- ¼ cup Chinese rice wine or dry sherry

- 2 tablespoons Worcestershire sauce

Directions

1. Combine the soy sauce, rice wine, and Worcestershire sauce in a small saucepan. Stir in the sugar. Bring to a boil, then cool. For best results, do not serve for 2 hours, to give the flavors time to blend.

Sweet and Sour Sauce with Tomato Paste

Ingredients

- ⅔ cup pineapple juice

- ¼ cup sugar

- ⅓ cup red wine vinegar

- ¼ cup tomato paste

Directions

1. Warm the pineapple juice and red wine vinegar in a small saucepan on low heat. Add the sugar, stirring to dissolve. Add the tomato paste and bring to a boil, stirring to make a smooth sauce. Keep warm on low heat until ready to serve.

Sweet and Sour Sauce

Ingredients

- 2 tablespoons cornstarch
- 6 teaspoons Worcestershire sauce
- 4 tablespoons water
- ½ cup brown sugar
- 1 cup pineapple juice
- ⅛ teaspoon ground ginger
- 4 tablespoons cider vinegar
- ⅛ teaspoon ground coriander
- 3 teaspoons soy sauce

Directions

1. Dissolve the cornstarch in the water and set aside. Combine the pineapple juice, cider vinegar, soy sauce, and Worcestershire sauce and set aside.

2. In a small saucepan, melt the brown sugar over low heat, stirring continuously. Add the pineapple juice mixture. Turn up the heat and bring to a boil.

3. Give the cornstarch and water mixture a quick stir and add to the sauce, stirring to thicken. Stir in the ground ginger and the coriander. Remove from the heat. Serve immediately, or prepare several hours ahead of time to give the flavors a chance to blend.

Teriyaki Marinade

Ingredients

- 1 garlic clove
- 2 teaspoons sugar

- ½ cup soy sauce

- 1 teaspoon ginger, chopped

- 3 tablespoons mirin (Japanese rice wine)

Directions

1. Smash and peel the garlic clove. Combine all the ingredients. For best results, make ahead of time to give the flavors a chance to blend.

Balsamic Vinegar Marinade

Ingredients

- 2 garlic cloves

- 1 teaspoon liquid honey

- 3 tablespoons balsamic vinegar

- ½ teaspoon prepared mustard

Directions

1. Smash, peel, and chop the garlic cloves. Combine all the ingredients. Marinate the meat for at least 1 hour before using in the fondue.

Marinated Cheese Cubes

Ingredients

- 2 garlic cloves

- 2 sprigs thyme, chopped

- 4 sprigs parsley

- 1 teaspoon sugar

- ½ cup vegetable oil

- Pinch of cayenne, optional

- ½ cup balsamic vinegar

- 1 pound sharp Cheddar cheese

Directions

1. Smash, peel, and chop the garlic cloves. Chop the parsley sprigs until you have 4 tablespoons.

2. Combine the vegetable oil, balsamic vinegar, garlic, chopped parsley, thyme, sugar, and cayenne in a bowl. Pour into a jar and shake well.

3. Cut the cheese into cubes. Lay out the cubes flat in a shallow glass dish and pour the marinade over. Cover and refrigerate overnight. Use as called for in the recipe.

Lemony Ginger Marinade

Ingredients

- ½ cup white wine

- 1 teaspoon ground ginger

- 2 tablespoons plus 2 tea-spoons lemon juice

- 1 teaspoon dried dill seeds

- 2 teaspoons brown sugar

Directions

1. Combine all the ingredients. Let the marinade sit, covered and refrigerated, at least 1 hour before using.

Quick and Easy Teriyaki Marinade

Ingredients

- 2 large slices ginger

- 2 tablespoons brown sugar

- ½ cup soy sauce

Directions

1. Grate the ginger finely until you have 2 teaspoons. Combine all the ingredients. Toss with the meat or seafood in a shallow glass dish and refrigerate.

Mediterranean Chicken Marinade

Ingredients

- 2 medium garlic cloves

- 1½ teaspoons fresh tarragon leaves

- ½ cup olive oil

- 2 tablespoons plus 1 teaspoon lemon juice

2. Smash and peel the garlic cloves. Combine all the ingredients. Use a pastry brush to baste the chicken with the marinade. For best results, marinate the chicken for at least 1 hour before cooking in the fondue.

Spunky Red Wine Vinegar Marinade

Ingredients

- ¾ cup red wine vinegar

- 3 teaspoons brown sugar

- 1 tablespoon Dijon mustard

- ¼ cup vegetable oil

- ½ teaspoon freshly squeezed ginger juice

Directions

1. Combine all the ingredients. Place the meat in a shallow glass dish or zipper-lock plastic bag and pour the marinade over.

Sweet and Sour Marinade

Ingredients

- 2 tablespoons vegetable oil

- 4 teaspoons brown sugar

- 4 tablespoons rice vinegar

- 1 teaspoon ginger, chopped

- 1½ teaspoons light soy sauce

Directions

1. Combine all the ingredients. Place the meat in a shallow glass dish, toss with the marinade, and refrigerate for at least 1 hour.

Basic Red Wine Marinade

Ingredients

- ⅓ cup red wine

- ½ teaspoon fresh thyme leaves, chopped

- 2 teaspoons lemon juice

- 2 tablespoons olive oil

Directions

1. Combine all the ingredients. Toss the beef in the marinade and refrigerate for at least 1 hour before cooking in the fondue.

Spicy Seafood Marinade

Ingredients

- 1½ teaspoons fresh ground white pepper
- 1½ teaspoons white sugar
- 4 tablespoons lemon juice
- 1½ teaspoons fresh ground black pepper

Directions

1. Combine all the ingredients. Brush on 1¼–1½ pounds of fresh or frozen fish or shellfish.

Dry Mustard and Chili Rub

Ingredients

- ½ cup dry mustard
- 1 tablespoon chili powder
- 2 tablespoons garlic powder
- 1 tablespoon cumin

Directions

1. Combine all the ingredients. Store in a sealed container until ready to use.

Instant Tandoori Rub

Ingredients

- 2 tablespoons ground coriander
- 2 teaspoons ground ginger
- 2 tablespoons ground cumin
- 1 teaspoon sugar
- 2 tablespoons ground cayenne pepper
- ¼ teaspoon garlic powder, or to taste

Directions

1. Combine all the ingredients. Store in a sealed container until ready to use.

Simple Chicken Rub

- 2 tablespoons paprika

- ½ teaspoon salt

- ½ teaspoon pepper

Directions

1. Combine all the ingredients. Store in a sealed container until ready to use.

Tempura Batter

Ingredients

- 1 egg, refrigerated

- 1 cup flour

- 1 cup ice-cold water, divided

- Black pepper, as desired

Directions

1. Combine the egg with fl cup cold water. Slowly stir in the flour, adding as much of the remaining ¼ cup of water as is necessary, until the batter has the thin, runny consistency of pancake batter. Add the black pepper if desired. Do not worry about lumps of flour in the batter. For best results, use immediately.

Japanese Beer Batter

Ingredients

- 1 teaspoon baking soda

- 2 teaspoons Worcestershire sauce Black pepper to taste

- 1 cup flour

- 3 teaspoons lemon juice

- 1 cup cold Japanese beer

Directions

1. Sift the baking soda into the flour. Stir in the lemon juice and Worcestershire sauce. Add the fresh ground black pepper.

2. Slowly pour in the beer and mix until the batter has the consistency of heavy cream. Do not add the entire cup if it's not needed. Allow the batter to rest in the refrigerator for 30 minutes before using.

Basic Batter

Ingredients

- 1 teaspoon baking soda
- ½ teaspoon cayenne pepper
- 1 cup flour
- 1 cup soda water
- 2 tablespoons vegetable oil
- Freshly ground black pepper to taste

Directions

1. Sift the baking soda into the flour. Stir in the vegetable oil, black pepper, and cayenne pepper.

2. Slowly add the soda water until you have a batter similar in texture to pancake batter. Feel free to adjust the amount of water or flour to obtain the right consistency. Allow the batter to rest in the refrigerator for 30 minutes before using.

Quick and Easy Batter

Ingredients

- 1 teaspoon baking soda
- 1 tablespoon vegetable oil
- 1 cup flour
- ¾ cup beer, preferably flat

Directions

1. Sift the baking soda into the flour, and stir in the vegetable oil. Slowly add ½ cup of the beer, stirring. Add as much of the remaining ¼ cup of beer as is necessary to form a thick batter that is not too runny.

Herbed Seafood Batter

Ingredients

- 2 teaspoons baking soda

- 2 sprigs fresh thyme

- 2 cups flour

- $1/8$ teaspoon each of salt and pepper

- 2 tablespoons vegetable oil

- 2 sprigs baby dill leaves, torn into small pieces

- 4 teaspoons lemon juice

- 1½ cups beer, preferably flat

Directions

1. Sift the baking soda into the flour. Stir in the vegetable oil. Add the dill and thyme leaves and the salt and pepper. Stir in the lemon juice.

2. Slowly add 1¼ cups beer, stirring to form a batter that is thick and drops off the spoon but is not runny. Add the remaining ¼ cup of beer if needed. Use as called for in the recipe.

Homemade Chicken Broth

Ingredients

- 1 3-pound stewing chicken

- 16 cups water

- 1 parsnip

- 3 parsley sprigs

- 1 carrot

- Salt and pepper to taste

- 1 celery stalk

Directions

1. Rinse the chicken thoroughly and pat dry. Wash and coarsely chop the parsnip, carrot, and celery.

2. Bring the water to a boil. Add the chicken, vegetables, and parsley to the water and bring to a boil. Skim off the foam that rises to the top. Stir in the salt and pepper. Reduce the heat and

simmer, uncovered, for another 1½ hours, occasionally skimming off the foam that rises to the top. Taste and add more seasonings if desired. Remove the **solid ingredients and strain.**

Vietnamese Beef Broth

Ingredients

- 2 garlic cloves
- 3 slices ginger
- 2 green onions
- 3 teaspoons hot chili sauce
- 5 cups beef broth
- 4½ teaspoons fish sauce
- 1 cup red wine

Directions

1. Smash and peel the garlic and roughly chop the green onions.

2. Combine all the ingredients in large saucepan and bring to a boil. Transfer enough broth to fill the fondue pot about ⅔ full. Set the fondue pot on the burner, with enough heat to keep the broth simmering throughout the meal. Keep the remaining broth warm on the stove to use as needed.

Asian Chicken Broth

Ingredients

- 4 pounds chicken wings, backs, and necks
- 16 cups water
- 1 tablespoon rice vinegar
- 1 garlic clove
- 2 green onions
- 4 slices ginger

Directions

1. Rinse the chicken thoroughly and dry. Smash and peel the garlic.

2. Add the chicken, green onions, ginger, and garlic to the water and bring to a boil. Skim off the foam. Turn down the heat and simmer the broth, covered, for another 1½ hours, skimming off any foam. Stir in the rice vinegar. Remove the solid ingredients and strain the soup through a sieve to remove much of the extra fat.

Chinese Beef Broth

Ingredients

- 6 cups beef broth
- 4 small slices ginger
- ½ cup soy sauce
- 2 tablespoons sherry
- 1 green onion, chopped
- ½ teaspoon five-spice powder

Directions

1. Combine all the ingredients in a large saucepan and bring to a boil. Transfer enough broth to fill the fondue pot about ⅔ full. Set the fondue pot on the burner, with enough heat to keep the broth simmering throughout the meal. Keep the remaining broth warm on the stove to use as needed.

Vegetable Broth

- 4 garlic cloves
- 2 tablespoons vegetable oil
- 1 large yellow onion
- 12 cups water
- 2 celery stalks
- 2 bay leaves
- 2 large carrots
- 2 sprigs thyme
- 1 green bell pepper

- ¼ cup fresh parsley

Directions

1. Smash, peel, and chop the garlic. Chop the onion without removing the peel. Chop the celery and carrots into chunks. Cut the green pepper in half, remove the seeds, and chop into chunks.

2. Heat the oil in a large saucepan. Add the chopped onion, garlic, and pepper and cook until the onion is tender and the garlic is aromatic.

3. Add the water, carrots, celery, bay leaves, thyme, and parsley. Bring to a boil, and then simmer on low heat, covered, for at least 1 hour. Remove the ingredients and strain the broth.

Simple Beef Broth

Ingredients

- 1 green onion

- 5 cups water

- 1 garlic clove

- 2 cups beef broth

Directions

1. Chop the green onion into thirds. Smash and peel the garlic. Combine the green onion and garlic with the water and beef broth. Bring all the ingredients to a boil. Simmer for 5 minutes before using in the fondue.

Basic Mongolian Hot Pot Broth

Ingredients

- 1 green onion

- 1 tablespoon rice wine or dry sherry

- 2½ cups Asian Chicken Broth or storebought chicken broth

- 2 slices ginger (about ½ tea-spoon)

- 3½ cups water

Directions

1. Chop the green onion into thirds. Combine all the ingredients and bring to a boil. Simmer for 5 minutes before using in the fondue.

Fish Broth

Ingredients

- 2 carrots

- 3 pounds fish heads and bones

- 2 parsnips

- 2 celery stalks

- 2 bay leaves

- ½ small yellow onion

- ¼ teaspoon celery salt

- 12 cups water

- Salt and pepper to taste

Directions

1. Chop the carrots, parsnips, and celery into chunks. Peel and coarsely chop the onion.

2. Bring the water to a boil. Combine the vegetables with the fish heads and bones, bay leaves, celery salt, and salt and pepper. Simmer for 1 hour. Cool and strain

Classic Beef Bourguignonne

Ingredients

- 1¾ pounds beef sirloin

- Quick and Easy Blender

- 5 cups oil, or as needed

- Hollandaise Sauce

- Béarnaise Sauce

- ¼ cup hot chili powder

Directions

1. Cut the meat into bite-sized cubes, approximately ¾ inch thick.

2. Add the oil to the fondue pot, making sure it is not more than half full. Heat the pot on a stove element over medium-high heat.

3. When the oil is hot, move the fondue pot to the table and set up the burner. Set out the béarnaise sauce, hollandaise sauce, and ground hot chili powder in small bowls. Use dipping forks to spear the beef cubes. Cook briefly in the hot oil and then dip into the sauces or seasoning. Add other condiments as desired.

Spicy Beef Bourguignonne

Ingredients

- 1¾ pounds flank sirloin steak
- ¾ cup freshly ground white pepper
- 1 sprig tarragon, finely minced
- 5 cups oil, or as needed
- Curried Yogurt

Directions

1. Cut the meat into cubes approximately ¾ inch thick. Mix with the minced tarragon and set aside.

2. Add the oil to the fondue pot, making sure it is not more than half full. Heat the pot on a stove element over medium-high heat.

3. When the oil is hot, move the fondue pot to the table and set up the burner. Set out the ground white pepper and Curried Yogurt in small bowls for dipping. Add other condiments such as horseradish, pickles, and onions as desired.

4. Use dipping forks to spear the beef cubes. Cook briefly in the hot oil and then dip into the seasoning and/or sauce.

Beef Kebabs

Ingredients

- 1½ pounds beef tenderloin
- Speedy Garlic Mayonnaise
- 5 cups oil, or as needed
- Mint and Cilantro Chutney
- Fried Mushrooms

*

1. Cut the meat into bite-sized cubes, approximately ¾ inch thick.

2. Add the oil to the fondue pot, making sure it is not more than half full. Heat the pot on a stove element over medium-high heat.

3. When the oil is hot, move the fondue pot to the table and set up the burner. Set out the chutney and the garlic mayonnaise in serving bowls. Set out metal skewers with wooden handles instead of dipping forks. Invite guests to place 2 beef cubes and 2 mushroom slices on each skewer. Cook the food briefly and eat with the chutney and mayonnaise.

Fondue au Boeuf

Ingredients

- 2 pounds beef sirloin

- 5 cups oil, or as needed

- Spunky Red Wine Vinegar Marinade

- ¼ cup fresh cracked black pepper, or as needed

- 2 shallots

Directions

1. Cut the meat into bite-sized cubes, approximately ¾ inch thick. Place the meat in a glass dish and pour the marinade over. Peel the shallots, chop, and add to the meat. Marinate the meat in the refrigerator for at least 2 hours. Remove excess marinade.

2. Add the oil to the fondue pot, making sure it is not more than half full. Heat the pot on a stove element over medium-high heat.

3. When the oil is hot, move the fondue pot to the table and set up the burner. Set out the fresh cracked black pepper in a serving bowl. Use dipping forks to spear the beef cubes and cook briefly in the hot oil, then dip into the cracked black pepper.

Meatballs with Basil

Ingredients

- 4 fresh basil leaves

- 2 teaspoons ground coriander

- 8 ounces ground beef

- 1 teaspoon ground cumin

- ¼ teaspoon celery salt

- 2 teaspoons ground cinnamon

- 1 tablespoon onion, chopped

- ¼ cup plain yogurt

- 1 cup cooked rice

- ¼ cup sour cream

- 2 tablespoons ground cardamom

- 4½ cups oil, or as necessary

Directions

1. Chop the fresh basil leaves. With your hands, mix together the ground beef, basil leaves, celery salt, onion, and 2 tablespoons of the cooked rice. Shape the ground beef mixture into 9 meatballs the size of golf balls. Roll the ground beef balls into the remainder of the cooked rice so that each ball is well covered.

2. Blend together the ground cardamom, ground coriander, ground cumin, and ground cinnamon. Combine the yogurt and sour cream. Add 2 teaspoons of the blended spices to the yogurt mixture. Store the remainder of the spice mixture in a sealed container to use another time.

3. Add the oil to the fondue pot, making sure it is not more than half full. Heat the pot on a stove element over medium-high heat.

4. When the oil is hot, move the fondue pot to the table and set up the burner. Using metal skewers with wooden handles, skewer the meatballs so that the skewer comes out the other side of the meatball. Cook the meatball in the hot oil for 4 to 5 minutes, until the rice is browned and the meat is cooked through. Serve with the spiced yogurt mixture for dipping.

Marinated Tomatoes

Ingredients

- 4 tomatoes

- 2 tablespoons water

- 2 green onions

- 1 teaspoon sugar

- ¼ cup olive oil

- 2 teaspoons cracked coriander

- 2 tablespoons lemon juice

- 1 tablespoon cranberry juice, optional

- 2 tablespoons balsamic vinegar

Directions

1. Peel the tomatoes and cut into thin slices. Thinly slice the green onions.

2. Whisk together the olive oil, lemon juice, balsamic vinegar, water, sugar, coriander, and cranberry juice. Place in a jar and shake well to blend the ingredients. If not using the marinade immediately, seal the jar and refrigerate until ready to use.

3. Pour the marinade over the tomatoes and green onions.

Oriental Vegetable Salad with Mediterranean Dressing

Ingredients

- 1 8-ounce can bamboo shoots

- ½ teaspoon sugar

- 1 red pepper

- Fresh ground black pepper to taste

- 1 garlic clove

- 2 tablespoons olive oil

- Parsley sprigs

- 1 tablespoon balsamic vinegar

Directions

1. Rinse the bamboo shoots in warm running water and drain thoroughly. Remove the stem and

seeds from the red pepper and cut into thin strips. Smash, peel, and mince the garlic. Place the vegetables in a bowl.

2. Combine the olive oil, balsamic vinegar, sugar, and black pepper. Toss with the vegetables. Garnish with the parsley.

Batter-Fried Broccoli

Ingredients

- ¾ pound broccoli
- 4 cups oil for deep-frying
- ¼ cup flour
- Tempura Batter

Directions

1. Steam the broccoli and drain thoroughly. Chop into pieces so that approximately 1 inch of the stalk is connected to the floweret. This will make it easier to keep the broccoli from sliding off the dipping fork into the hot oil. Lightly dust the broccoli with the flour.

2. Add the oil to the fondue pot, making sure it is not more than half full. Heat the pot over medium-high heat. When the oil is hot, move the fondue pot to the table, set up the burner, and maintain the heat.

3. To cook, place a broccoli piece on a dipping fork and coat with batter. Feel free to use your fingers to lightly cover the broccoli with the batter. Dip into the hot oil and cook briefly until the coating turns golden brown. Drain on paper towels or a tempura rack.

Fried Mushrooms

Ingredients

- 30 mushrooms
- 4½ cups oil, or as needed

Directions

1. Wipe the mushrooms clean with a damp cloth. Dry and cut into slices approximately ½ inch thick.

2. Add the oil to the fondue pot, making sure it is not more than half full. Heat the pot on a stove element over medium-high heat.

3. When the oil is hot, move the fondue pot to the table, set on the burner, and maintain the heat. Use a dipping fork to cook the mushroom slices briefly in the hot oil until golden. Drain on paper towels or a tempura rack.

Autumn Harvest Vegetables

Ingredients

- 6 ounces broccoli

- 4½ cups oil, or as needed Basic Batter

- 4 potatoes

- 12 fresh large mushrooms

- Fresh ground black pepper and white pepper

- ¼ cup cornstarch

Directions

1. Steam the broccoli, and drain thoroughly. Boil the potatoes on medium-low heat for about 15 minutes, until they can be pierced with a fork but are not too soft. Wipe the mushrooms with a damp cloth.

2. Cut the steamed broccoli into pieces so that approximately 1 inch of the stem is attached to the floweret. Cut the potato lengthwise into slices approximately ¾ inch thick. Cut the mushrooms into slices approximately ½ inch thick. Dust the prepared vegetables lightly with the cornstarch.

3. Add the oil to the fondue pot, making sure it is not more than half full. Heat the pot on a stove element over medium-high heat.

4. When the oil is hot, move the fondue pot to the table, set up the burner, and maintain the heat. Using a dipping fork, dip the vegetables into the batter and cook briefly in the hot oil until they turn golden brown. Remove from the dipping fork and drain on paper towels or a tempura rack. Dip into the black and white pepper.

Roasted Red Peppers

Ingredients

- 3 red bell peppers
- 1 teaspoon balsamic vinegar
- 2 yellow bell peppers
- 1 teaspoon olive oil
- 1 orange bell pepper

Directions

1. Place the peppers side down (not standing up) on a broiling pan. Brush the top side of the peppers with the balsamic vinegar. Turn over and brush the other side with the olive oil. Broil the peppers for about 20 minutes, turning frequently, until the skins are blackened and charred.

2. Place the peppers in a sealed plastic bag. Leave the peppers in the bag for at least 10 minutes. Remove from the bag and peel off the skins. Remove the stems and the seeds. To serve, cut into cubes or lengthwise into strips.

Roasted Pepper Dip

Ingredients

- 1 garlic clove
- ½ teaspoon sugar
- 3 tablespoons onion, chopped
- ½ teaspoon lemon juice
- 2 tablespoons olive oil
- ¼ teaspoon ground cumin, or to taste
- 2 red bell peppers

Directions

1. Smash, peel, and chop the garlic clove. Cook the garlic and onion in the olive oil.

2. Roast the red peppers (see Roasted Red Peppers), remove the peel and seeds, and cut into cubes. Process with the garlic and onion in the blender. Add the sugar, lemon juice, and

ground cumin. Process again briefly, keeping the texture a bit chunky, like a salsa.

Asian Vegetables with Vinaigrette Dressing

Ingredients

- 1 8-ounce can baby corn

- 1 teaspoon sugar

- 1 red bell pepper

- 1 teaspoon rice vinegar

- ½ cup mung bean sprouts

- ¼ teaspoon ginger juice, or to taste

- 1 tablespoon olive oil

- 2 tablespoons soy sauce

Directions

1. Rinse the baby corn in warm running water. Wash the red pepper and mung bean sprouts. Drain all the vegetables well. Remove the stem and seeds from the red pepper and cut into cubes. Place in a large bowl.

2. Combine the olive oil, soy sauce, sugar, rice vinegar, and ginger juice. Toss the vegetables with the dressing. Let the salad sit for about 30 minutes before serving.

Sweet Peppers and Herbs

Ingredients

- 1 potato, boiled

- 1 tablespoon fresh parsley, chopped

- 1 tablespoon balsamic vinegar

- 1 teaspoon olive oil

- 2 mint leaves, chopped

- 3 tablespoons onion, chopped

- 2 large red bell peppers, roasted

- 1 garlic clove, minced

- 1 tablespoon fresh cilantro, chopped

Directions

1. Cut the potato into thin strips. Mix together the balsamic vinegar, olive oil, chopped onion, minced garlic, cilantro, parsley, and mint leaves. Add to the potato strips, tossing.

2. Peel the roasted peppers, cut off the stems, and remove the seeds. Cut the peppers into thin strips. Combine with the other ingredients. Cover and refrigerate until ready to serve.

Fried Mashed Potatoes

Ingredients

- 4 medium potatoes
- ¼ teaspoon salt
- 3 tablespoons butter or margarine
- ½ cup flour
- ⅛ teaspoon garlic powder
- ½ cup plus 3 tablespoons milk, divided
- 5 cups oil, or as needed
- ¼ teaspoon paprika

Directions

1. Wash and peel the potatoes. Cook in boiling salted water until they are tender and pierce easily with a fork.

2. Place the potatoes in a bowl and add the butter or margarine, 3 tablespoons milk, paprika, and a pinch of salt. Use a potato masher or fork to mash the potatoes until they are fluffy. Roll into balls. Place on a tray lined with wax paper and freeze overnight.

3. To prepare the batter, mix together the flour, garlic powder, pepper, and remaining salt. Stir in 1 tablespoon vegetable oil. Slowly add ½ cup milk, stirring constantly, until it forms a runny batter.

4. Add the oil to the fondue pot, making sure it is not more than half full. Heat the pot on a stove element over medium-high heat. When the oil is hot, move the fondue pot to the table and set up the burner. Keep the heat high.

5. Roll the mashed potato balls in the batter and drop into the hot oil. Cook for about 4 minutes, turning occasionally, until they turn a deep golden brown and are cooked through. Remove with a slotted spoon and drain on paper towels.

Fried Potato Sticks

Ingredients

- 4 large potatoes
- Freshly ground black pepper and white pepper
- 5 cups oil, or as needed

Directions

1. Boil the potatoes for about 15 minutes on medium-low heat, until they can be pierced with a fork but are not too soft. Drain thoroughly, and cut lengthwise into pieces approximately ¾ inch thick.

2. Add the oil to the fondue pot, making sure it is not more than half full. Heat the pot on a stove element over medium-high heat. When the oil is hot, move the fondue pot to the table and set up the burner. Keep the heat high.

3. Using a dipping fork, dip the potato slices briefly into the oil. Drain on paper towels or a tempura rack. Season with black or white pepper as desired before eating.

Fried Potato Skins

Ingredients

- 4 baking potatoes
- ¼ teaspoon paprika
- ¼ teaspoon ground white pepper
- 4½ cups oil, or as needed

Directions

1. Bake the potatoes at 425°F until they are tender and pierce easily with a fork. Cool. Cut the potatoes in half. Cut each half lengthwise into 3 to 4 sections. Scoop out most of the pulp, so that only ⅛ to ¼ inch remains. Discard the pulp or use in another recipe. Sprinkle half the potato skins with the ground white pepper, and the remaining half with the paprika. Add

more seasoning if desired.

2. Add the oil to the fondue pot, making sure it is not more than half full. Heat the pot on a stove element over medium-high heat. When the oil is hot, move the fondue pot to the table and set up the burner. Keep the heat high.

3. Using a dipping fork, briefly dip the potato slices into the oil until browned.

Milk Bathed Onion Rings

Ingredients

- 1 large yellow onion
- ½ cup cornstarch
- ½ teaspoon paprika
- Tempura Batter
- 1 cup milk
- 4½ cups oil, or as needed

Directions

1. Peel the onion and cut into rings. Toss with the paprika. Soak in the milk for at least 1 hour, making sure all the onion pieces are covered.

2. Drain the onion pieces and dust with the cornstarch. Coat with the batter.

3. Add the oil to the fondue pot, making sure it is not more than half full. Heat the pot on a stove element over medium-high heat. When the oil is hot, move the fondue pot to the table and set up the burner. Keep the heat high.

4. Drop the battered onion rings into the oil. Cook briefly, turning occasionally, until they turn golden brown. Remove and drain on paper towels.

Pepper Medley

Ingredients

- 2 red bell peppers
- 4 cups Vegetable Broth
- 2 green bell peppers

- 2 orange bell peppers

- ½ cup soy sauce

Directions

1. Wash the peppers and drain thoroughly. Remove the seeds and stems, and cut into bite-sized cubes.

2. Heat the broth in the fondue pot over a stove element. Bring to the table and set up the burner. Add the peppers and simmer until tender. Remove the peppers with a slotted spoon. If desired, ladle the broth into individual serving bowls. Serve with the soy sauce for dipping.

Garden Vegetables with White Sauce

Ingredients

- 2 tablespoons olive oil

- 1 cup snow peas

- ¼ onion, peeled and chopped

- 1 cup baby carrots

- 2 cups long-grain rice

- 2 green peppers

- 5 cups Homemade Chicken Broth (), divided

- White Sauce for Vegetables

Directions

1. Heat the olive oil in a frying pan on low heat. Add the chopped onion and cook until soft. Add the rice and sauté for 5 minutes until it turns shiny and is heated through.

2. Add 3 cups of the broth. To cook the rice, bring to a boil, uncovered. Cover, turn down the heat, and cook until cooked through.

3. Wash the snow peas, carrots, and green peppers; drain thoroughly. Cut the peppers in half, remove the seeds and stems, and cut into bite-sized cubes.

4. Heat the remaining 2 cups of broth in a fondue pot over a stove element. Bring to the table and set up the burner. Add the vegetables to the broth, using a dipping basket if you have one. Simmer the vegetables until tender. If not using a dipping basket, remove with a slotted

spoon.

5. Serve the vegetables with the warmed sauce for dipping. Eat with the rice. At the end of the meal, serve the cooked broth if desired.

French Green Beans with Fondue Béchamel Sauce

Ingredients

- Fondue Béchamel Sauce

- 2 cups Homemade Chicken Broth

- 3 cups canned French-style green beans

Directions

1. Warm the sauce on low heat, without allowing to come to a boil.

2. Drain the green beans. Bring the broth to a boil. Add the green beans and gently simmer for about 10 minutes.

3. Pour the fondue sauce over the beans and serve.

Cream of Celery Soup

Ingredients

- 1 stalk celery

- 2 10-ounce cans cream of celery soup

- 1 green onion

- 1 tablespoon butter or margarine

- 10 ounces chicken broth

- ¼ cup yellow onion, chopped

- 10 ounces water

- Salt and pepper to taste

Directions

1. Wash the celery. Cut the celery and green onion into 1-inch slices on the diagonal.

2. On a stove element, melt the butter in the fondue pot, add the chopped onion, and cook until

tender. Mix in the cream of celery soup, chicken broth, and water and heat through. Season with the salt and pepper.

3. Bring the fondue pot to the table and set on the stand. Add the celery and green onion to the soup and simmer briefly until tender. Allow everyone to serve themselves or ladle the soup into individual serving bowls.

Tomato Soup Fondue

Ingredients

- 12 ounces beef broth
- ¼ teaspoon celery salt
- 8 ounces water
- Salt and pepper to taste
- 2 10-ounce cans tomato soup
- Toasted Pita Chips
- 8 ounces Cheddar cheese, shredded

Directions

1. Bring the beef broth and water to a boil in the fondue pot on the stove. Stir in the tomato soup and heat through. Keeping the heat on medium-low, gradually stir in the shredded Cheddar cheese, a handful at a time. Stir in the celery salt and salt and pepper.

2. Bring the fondue pot to the table and set up the burner. Allow everyone to serve themselves or ladle the soup into individual serving bowls. Dip the pita chips into the soup.

Fried Asparagus and Zucchini

Ingredients

- 2 zucchini
- Speedy Garlic Mayonnaise
- 1 pound asparagus spears
- 4 cups oil, or as needed
- ½ cup soy sauce

Directions

1. Wash the zucchini and dry thoroughly. Cut on the diagonal into pieces at least ½ inch thick. Blanch the asparagus briefly in boiling water. Drain thoroughly, and cut into 2-inch pieces.

2. Add the oil to the fondue pot, making sure it is not more than half full. Heat the pot on a stove element over medium-high heat. When the oil is hot, move the fondue pot to the table and set up the burner.

3. Spear the vegetables with a dipping fork and cook briefly in the hot oil. Serve with Garlic Mayonnaise and soy sauce for dipping.

Vegetable Spring Rolls

Ingredients

- 1 cup fresh mung bean sprouts
- 2 teaspoons water
- ½ teaspoon sugar
- ½ carrot
- 1 teaspoon soy sauce
- 4 dried Chinese mushrooms
- 5 cups oil, or as needed
- 1 tablespoon bamboo shoots, shredded
- 8–10 spring roll wrappers
- 4 tablespoons cornstarch mixed with 2 tablespoons water
- 2 tablespoons plus 1 teaspoon red pepper, finely diced
- 1 tablespoon plus 1 teaspoon oyster sauce

Directions

1. Wash or rinse all the vegetables and drain thoroughly, particularly the mung bean sprouts. Grate the carrot until you have 2 tablespoons plus 1 teaspoon. Soak the dried Chinese mushrooms in warm water for at least 20 minutes to soften. Squeeze out the excess water, remove the stems, and thinly slice. Mix together the mung bean sprouts, grated carrot, mushrooms, bamboo shoots, and diced red pepper.

2. Mix together the oyster sauce, water, sugar, and soy sauce. Set aside.

3. Heat 1½ tablespoons vegetable oil in a frying pan. When oil is hot, add the vegetables. Mix in the sauce and bring to a boil.

4. To prepare the spring rolls, lay a wrapper in front of you so that it forms 2 triangles. Use your fingers to brush the edges of the wrapper with the cornstarch-and-water mixture. Place a full tablespoon of filling in the middle. Roll up the wrapper, tucking in the edges, and seal with more cornstarch and water. Prepare the remaining spring rolls in the same way.

5. Add the remaining oil as needed to the fondue pot, making sure it is not more than half full. Heat the pot on a stove element over medium-high heat. When the oil is hot, move the fondue pot to the table and set up the burner. Deep-fry the spring rolls, two at a time, until they turn golden (3 to 4 minutes). Drain on paper towels.

Tempura Vegetables

Ingredients

- 6 ounces lotus root
- Tempura Batter
- 1 pound daikon radish
- 4½ cups oil, or as needed
- 1 green pepper
- Yogurt and Dill Dressing
- 1 Western eggplant (about 10 ounces)
- ½ cup soy sauce, optional
- ⅓ cup flour

Directions

1. Wash all the vegetables. Cut the ends off the lotus root. Scrape the skin off the lotus root and daikon radish with a potato peeler, and cut into slices about ½ inch thick. Cut the green pepper in half, remove the stem and seeds, and cut into 1-inch cubes. Peel the eggplant and cut into sticks about ½ inch thick and 3 inches long.

2. Dust all the vegetables lightly with the flour before setting on the table for dipping. (Some flour will probably be left over.) Prepare the batter.

3. Add the oil to the fondue pot, making sure it is not more than half full. Heat the pot on a stove element over medium-high heat. When the oil is hot, move the fondue pot to the table and set up the burner.

4. Invite guests to spear the vegetables with a dipping fork and coat with the batter. Cook the vegetables in the hot oil until golden brown. Try to vary which vegetables are cooked to allow for different cooking times — the eggplant will take up to 4 minutes, while the peppers will cook quite quickly. Serve with the Yogurt and Dill Dressing and soy sauce for dipping.

Parsnip Soup

Ingredients

- 4 pears
- ¾ teaspoon curry powder
- 4 parsnips
- ¼ teaspoon salt
- ½ yellow onion
- Pepper to taste
- 1 garlic clove
- 2 tablespoons parsley, chopped
- 4 cups Vegetable Broth

Directions

1. Wash the pears, remove the stems, and cut into bite-sized pieces. Wash and peel the parsnips. Cut diagonally into ½-inch pieces. Peel and chop the onion. Smash, peel, and chop the garlic clove.

2. Heat the broth in the fondue pot over a stove element. Add the parsnips, onion, garlic, curry powder, salt, and pepper to the broth. Simmer for at least 15 minutes, or until parsnips are tender. Stir in the parsley.

3. Transfer the fondue pot to the table and set up the burner. Use dipping forks to spear the pears and dip into the soup.

Vegetable Medley

Ingredients

- ½ pound broccoli

- Vegetable Broth

- ½ pound cauliflower

- Lemon-Soy Dressing

- 2 carrots

- Sour Cream and Mustard Dip

- ½ green pepper

- ½ red pepper

Directions

1. Blanch the broccoli and cauliflower briefly in boiling water and drain thoroughly. Remove the stems and cut the flowerets into bite-sized pieces.

2. Peel and dice the carrots. Blanch briefly in boiling water and drain.

3. Cut the green and red peppers into bite-sized pieces.

4. Heat the broth in the fondue pot over a stove element. Bring to a boil and then transfer the fondue pot to the table and set up the burner. Use dipping forks to spear the vegetables and cook in the hot broth. Serve with the dressing and the dip.

Fried Three Mushrooms

Ingredients

- 20 fresh small mushrooms

- Horseradish with Sour Cream

- 6 portobello mushrooms

- 4 oyster mushrooms

- ½ cup balsamic vinegar

- 4½ cups oil, or as needed

Directions

1. Wipe the mushrooms with a damp cloth. If desired, remove the feathery "gills" from underneath the cap of the portobello and oyster mushrooms.

2. Remove the stems from all the mushrooms. Slice the small mushrooms. Cut the portobello and the oyster mushrooms into bite-sized squares or rectangles (this will give them a better surface area for cooking in hot oil).

3. Add the oil to the fondue pot, making sure it is not more than half full. Heat the pot on a stove element over medium-high heat. When the oil is hot, move the fondue pot to the table and set up the burner.

4. Spear the mushrooms with a dipping fork. Cook for approximately 20 seconds in the hot oil until the mushrooms are lightly browned but not burned. (If not cooked long enough, they can taste oily.) Drain on paper towels. Serve with the Horseradish with Sour Cream and balsamic vinegar for dipping.

Vegetables with Boiled Salad Dressing

Ingredients

- 4 carrots

- 4 eggs

- 4 celery stalks

- ½ cup sugar

- 2 tomatoes

- ½ teaspoon cayenne pepper

- 1 head romaine lettuce

- 2 tablespoons Dijon mustard

- 8 tablespoons butter

- ½ cup light cream or half-and-half

- ½ cup white vinegar

Directions

1. Wash all the vegetables and drain thoroughly. Peel the carrots and cut lengthwise into thin slices about 2 inches long. Cut the celery the same way. Cut the tomatoes into wedges.

Separate the romaine lettuce leaves. Arrange the carrots, celery, and tomato wedges on the lettuce and place on a large serving platter.

2. To prepare the boiled dressing, melt the butter in a small saucepan. Place the vinegar in the top half of a double boiler or in a metal bowl over water that is just barely simmering.

3. Slowly add the eggs and melted butter to the warmed vinegar. Whisk constantly until the mixture thickens (this can take several minutes). Once the mixture has thickened, whisk in the sugar, cayenne pepper, and Dijon mustard. Remove from the heat and whisk in the cream.

4. Pour the boiled dressing into a cheese fondue dish. Serve hot or cold. Use dipping forks to spear the salad vegetables and dip into the dressing

Mexican Fondue with Guacamole Dip

Ingredients

- ¾ pound Cheddar cheese

- 3 teaspoons lemon juice

- ¾ pound Monterey Jack cheese

- 1 tablespoon cornstarch

- 3 fresh green jalapeño peppers

- 3 tablespoons cognac

- 1 garlic clove

- 1 bag tortilla chips

- 1½ cups beer

- Guacamole

Directions

1. Shred the Cheddar and Monterey Jack cheeses. Wash the peppers, cut lengthwise, remove the seeds, and chop.

2. Smash the garlic, peel, and cut in half. Rub the inside of a medium saucepan with the garlic. Add the beer and warm on medium-low heat, being careful not to bring to a boil. When the beer has warmed, stir in the lemon juice.

3. Add the cheese, a handful at a time. Stir the cheese continually in a sideways figure eight pattern. Don't allow the fondue mixture to boil.

4. When the cheese is nearly melted, turn up the heat until it is just bubbling. Dissolve the cornstarch in 2 tablespoons of cognac and add to the fondue, stirring quickly to thicken. Add the remaining tablespoon of cognac. Transfer to a fondue pot and set on the burner. Serve with the tortilla chips for dipping and accompany with the Guacamole dip.

Bagna Cauda — Italian Fondue

Ingredients

- 1 small head broccoli
- 4 ounces anchovies
- 1 small head cauliflower
- 4 garlic cloves
- 2 cardoon stalks (or 2 celery stalks)
- 4 tablespoons butter
- ½ cup olive oil
- 1 fennel bulb
- 4 tablespoons cream
- 2 red peppers
- 1 loaf Italian bread, sliced
- 1 zucchini

Directions

1. Wash the vegetables. Blanch the broccoli, cauliflower, and cardoon stalks briefly in boiling water and drain thoroughly. Cut all the vegetables and fennel bulb into bite-sized pieces.

2. Drain and separate the anchovies. Smash, peel, and mince the garlic.

3. Melt the butter and keep warm on low heat.

4. Heat the olive oil in a frying pan over low heat. Add the garlic. Cook on low heat for a few minutes, and then add the anchovies. Continue to cook on low heat, gently mashing the anchovies and mixing together with the garlic. Add the melted butter. Stir in the cream.

5. Transfer the Bagna Cauda to a fondue pot and set on the burner. Serve with the vegetables — or with your own favorite combination of mixed vegetables — for dipping. Eat with the sliced bread.

Fondue Chinoise

Ingredients

- 2 pounds filet of beef
- Marvelous Mango Chutney
- Chinese Beef Broth
- Horseradish Cream
- Basic Chinese Hot Mustard (), prepared just before serving

Directions

1. Cut the beef into very thin slices, approximately 2 inches long.

2. Heat the broth on the stove and bring to a boil. Transfer enough broth to fill the fondue pot about ⅔ full. Set the fondue pot on the burner, with enough heat to keep the broth simmering throughout the meal. (Keep the remaining broth warm on the stove to use as needed.)

3. Invite guests to spear the sliced beef with a dipping fork and cook briefly in the broth until cooked according to individual taste. Serve with the Horseradish Cream and mustard for dipping. Eat with the chutney.

Marinated Fondue Chinoise

Ingredients

- 2 pounds beef flank steak
- 2 tablespoons sesame oil
- 1 green onion
- Chinese Beef Broth
- ¼ cup soy sauce
- Hot Pot Dip for Beef
- 3 tablespoons dry sherry

- Golden Hot Mustard

Directions

1. Cut the beef into very thin slices. Cut the green onion into thirds. Place the beef in a shallow glass dish and marinate the beef in the soy sauce, sherry, sesame oil, and green onion in the refrigerator for 1 hour.

2. Heat the broth on the stove and bring to a boil. Transfer enough broth to fill the fondue pot about ⅔ full. Set the fondue pot on the burner, with enough heat to keep the broth simmering throughout the meal. (Keep the remaining broth warm on the stove to use as needed.)

3. Spear the sliced beef with a dipping fork and cook briefly in the broth to individual taste. Serve with the dipping sauces.

Classic Mongolian Hot Pot

Ingredients

- 3 pounds lean lamb
- Extra Hot Pot Dipping Sauce
- 6 Chinese dried mushrooms
- 8 ounces cellophane noodles
- Nut-Free Hot Pot Dipping Sauce
- 1 head Napa cabbage
- 1 bunch fresh spinach (approximately ½ pound)
- 6 eggs
- Basic Mongolian Hot Pot Broth

Directions

1. Cut the lamb into paper thin slices, about 2½ inches long.

2. Soak the dried mushrooms in warm water for 20 minutes. Squeeze out the excess water and cut into thin slices. Soak the cellophane noodles in warm water to soften. Drain and cut into thirds for easier use.

3. Wash the cabbage, drain, and remove the stem. Cut each leaf in half lengthwise, and then

slice thinly. Wash the spinach and drain.

4. Heat the broth on the stove and bring to a boil. Add the dried mushrooms. Transfer enough broth to fill the fondue pot about ⅔ full. Set the fondue pot on the burner, with enough heat to keep the broth simmering throughout the meal. (Keep the remaining broth warm on the stove to use as needed.)

5. Invite guests to spear the sliced lamb with a dipping fork and cook briefly in the broth until cooked according to individual taste. Serve with the dipping sauces. When the lamb is gone, cook the noodles, cabbage, and spinach in the hot broth. When all the food is gone, poach the eggs in the broth.

Mixed Meat Hot Pot

Ingredients

- 2 teaspoons salt
- 1 bunch cilantro
- 1 pound fresh large shrimp, peeled and deveined
- Basic Mongolian Hot Pot Broth
- 1 pound fresh red snapper fillets
- 3 slices ginger
- Extra Hot Pot Dipping Sauce
- 2 skinless, boneless chicken breasts (about 8 ounces each)
- Sesame Dipping Paste
- 1 pound bok choy
- 1 egg
- 2 green onions

Directions

1. Dissolve the salt in 3 cups of warm water. Soak the shrimp in the water for 5 minutes. Drain and pat dry. Cut the red snapper and chicken breasts into thin strips.

2. Wash the vegetables and drain. Separate the bok choy stalks and leaves. Shred the leaves and cut the stalks into slices about 1 inch thick. Chop the green onions. Chop the cilantro and use

to garnish the shrimp.

3. Heat the broth on the stove and bring to a boil. Add the bok choy, green onions, and ginger. Bring to a boil again. Transfer enough broth to fill the fondue pot about ⅔ full. Set the fondue pot on the burner, with enough heat to keep the broth simmering throughout the meal. (Keep the remaining broth warm on the stove to use as needed.)

4. Ladle a small portion of the broth with vegetables into the soup bowls. Invite guests to use chopsticks or dipping forks to cook the chicken and seafood in the hot pot. Dip the cooked food in dipping sauces, or enjoy with the bowls of broth.

5. When the food is gone, swirl an egg into the broth to make egg drop soup. Serve each guest a bowl of the soup.

Provolone "Fonduta"

Ingredients

- 1 pound provolone cheese
- ½ teaspoon nutmeg
- 1¼ cups milk
- ¼ teaspoon cinnamon, or to taste
- 4 egg yolks
- ¼ cup half-and-half or light cream
- Salt and pepper to taste
- 1 loaf Italian bread, sliced and toasted
- 2 tablespoons butter

Directions

1. Finely dice the provolone cheese. Place the cheese and the milk in a saucepan and leave for 1 hour.

2. Heat the milk and cheese on low heat, without bringing to a boil, until the cheese turns creamy. Whisk in the egg yolks, half-and-half, and butter. Keep whisking until the mixture thickens, but not to the point where the egg starts scrambling. Stir in the nutmeg, cinnamon, and salt and pepper.

3. Transfer to a fondue pot and set on the burner. Serve with the toasted Italian bread for dipping.

Greek Fondue

Ingredients

- ¾ cup milk

- ¼ teaspoon dried oregano

- ¾ pound ricotta cheese

- ¼ teaspoon dried basil

- ½ pound feta cheese

- Toasted Pita Chips

- ¾ tablespoon cornstarch

- Bruschetta with Roma Tomatoes

- 1 garlic clove, peeled

- 2 teaspoons lemon juice

Directions

1. Mix ¼ cup of the milk with the ricotta cheese and set aside. Crumble the feta cheese and toss with the cornstarch. Cut the garlic in half. Rub the garlic around the inside of a medium saucepan. Discard. Add the remaining ½ cup of milk and warm on medium-low heat. Stir in the lemon juice. Add the ricotta cheese mixture and the feta cheese, stirring continuously. Don't let the cheese boil. When the cheese is fully melted, turn up the heat until it is just bubbling and starting to thicken. Stir in the oregano and basil. Serve with the pita chips and bruschetta for dipping.

Japanese Sukiyaki

Ingredients

- 16 ounces beef sirloin steak

- 10 oyster mushrooms

- 1 pound firm or medium-firm tofu

- 4 eggs

- 2 tablespoons cooking oil, or as needed

- 6 ounces cellophane noodles

- 1 small Napa cabbage

- Sukiyaki Sauce

Directions

1. Cut the beef into paper-thin slices, no more than 3 inches long. Drain the tofu and cut into cubes. Soak the noodles in warm water for 15 minutes to soften, and drain thoroughly. If desired, cut the noodles in half to make them more manageable. Wash the cabbage, drain, and shred the leaves. Wipe the mushrooms with a damp cloth, and cut into bite-sized pieces.

2. Set a sukiyaki pan or large electric frying pan in the middle of the table. When setting the table, make sure each guest has a small bowl containing a beaten egg.

3. Heat 2 tablespoons of oil in the pan. Brown the meat in the oil. Add the tofu, vegetables, mushrooms, and noodles. Pour the Sukiyaki Sauce over. Invite guests to use chopsticks to retrieve the cooked food and dip into the beaten egg.

Sukiyaki with Rice

Ingredients

- 1 small Napa cabbage

- 4 cups cooked rice

- 1 cup fresh mung bean sprouts

- 2 tablespoons vegetable oil, or as needed

- 10 fresh small mushrooms

- ¾ cup soy sauce

- 1 pound flank steak

- ¼ cup sake

- 1 block firm tofu

- 4 tablespoons sugar

Directions

1. Wash the cabbage and mung bean sprouts and drain thoroughly. Wipe the mushrooms with a

damp cloth. Slice the mushrooms and shred the cabbage leaves. Cut the steak into paper-thin slices, no more than 3 inches long. Drain the tofu and cut into cubes.

2. Give each guest a small bowl with 1 cup of the cooked rice to eat with the food. Set a sukiyaki pan or large electric frying pan in the middle of the table.

3. Heat the cooking oil in the pan. Add ½ of the beef and lightly braise it. Add ½ of the mushrooms, cabbage, and tofu, putting each in their own section. Add as much of the soy sauce, sake, and sugar as desired. When the food is almost cooked, add ½ of the bean sprouts. Either serve the cooked food to the guests or invite them to serve themselves. Repeat with the remaining half of the food. Eat with the cooked rice.

Spicy Hot Pot for a Crowd

Ingredients

- 2 teaspoons salt

- Extra Hot Pot Dipping Sauce

- 1 pound prawns or large shrimp, cleaned and deveined

- Nut-Free Hot Pot Dipping Sauce

- 3 large skinless, boneless chicken breasts (about 10 ounces each)

- 12 cups Basic Mongolian Hot Pot Broth

- 2 pounds fish fillets

- 4 garlic cloves, peeled

- 10 fresh oysters

- 4 tablespoons Worcestershire sauce

- 8 Chinese dried mushrooms

- 4 stalks celery

- 1 teaspoon hot chili sauce

- 2 bunches spinach

- 10 eggs

Directions

1. Dissolve the salt in 3 cups of warm water. Rinse the prawns in the water for 5 minutes, and

pat dry. Cut in half lengthwise. Cut the chicken and fish fillets into very thin slices. Shuck the oysters, rinse in warm water, and dry thoroughly.

2. Soak the dried mushrooms in warm water for 20 minutes to soften. Cut into thin slices. Wash the spinach and celery and drain thoroughly. Cut the celery into bite-sized pieces on the diagonal.

3. Place the chicken, seafood, celery, and spinach, on the table, along with dipping sauces. Give each guest an individual soup bowl.

4. Heat the broth on the stove with the mushrooms and garlic cloves and bring to a boil. Stir in the Worcestershire sauce and hot chili sauce. Transfer enough broth to fill the fondue pot about ⅔ full. Set the fondue pot on the burner, with enough heat to keep the broth simmering throughout the meal. (Keep the remaining broth warm on the stove to use as needed.)

5. Use chopsticks or dipping forks to cook the chicken, seafood, and celery in the hot pot. Dip the cooked food in dipping sauces, or enjoy with the bowls of broth. When the food is gone, add the spinach to the broth. Ladle out a small bowl for each guest. Poach the eggs in the remaining broth.

Shabu-Shabu

Ingredients

- 1 8-ounce can bamboo shoots
- Lemon-Soy Dressing
- 1 small Napa Cabbage
- Instant Dashi or Vegetable Broth (), as needed
- 4 leeks
- 2 large carrots
- 1 block medium-firm tofu
- 4 cups cooked rice
- 1½ pounds sirloin beef

Directions

1. Rinse the bamboo shoots in warm running water. Wash the cabbage, leeks, and carrots. Drain

all the vegetables thoroughly. Chop the leeks and shred the cabbage. Peel and dice the carrots.

2. Drain the tofu and cut into bite-sized cubes. Cut the beef into paper-thin slices. Arrange the meat, tofu, and vegetables separately on a large platter. Serve the Lemon-Soy Dressing in individual serving bowls.

3. Heat the dashi or broth on the stove and bring to a boil. Transfer enough broth to fill the fondue pot about ⅔ full. Set the fondue pot on the burner, with enough heat to keep the broth simmering throughout the meal. (Keep the remaining broth warm on the stove to use as needed.)

4. Invite guests to cook the meat, tofu, and all the vegetables except for the bamboo shoots in the broth, and then dip into the dressing. Replenish the broth as needed. Serve the rice with the food. When the food has been eaten, add the bamboo shoots to the broth, cook briefly, and then ladle out the soup.

Shabu-Shabu with Noodles

Ingredients

- 2 ounces cellophane noodles

- Instant Dashi or Vegetable Broth (), as needed

- 2 leeks

- 2 carrots

- 1 small Napa Cabbage

- ½ cup grated daikon radish

- 10 shiitake mushrooms

- 1½ pounds sirloin beef

- Sesame Dipping Paste (), prepared in advance to allow flavors to blend

Directions

1. Soak the cellophane noodles in warm water to soften. Drain thoroughly and chop into quarters. Wash the vegetables and drain thoroughly. Chop the leeks and peel and dice the carrots. Shred the cabbage. Wipe the mushrooms with a damp cloth and slice thinly.

2. Cut the beef into paper-thin slices. Arrange the meat, vegetables, and noodles separately on a large platter. If desired, set out the sesame dip in individual serving bowls.

3. Heat the dashi or broth on the stove and bring to a boil. Transfer enough broth to fill the fondue pot about ⅔ full. Set the fondue pot on the burner, with enough heat to keep the broth simmering throughout the meal. (Keep the remaining broth warm on the stove to use as needed.)

4. Invite guests to cook all the meat and vegetables and then dip into the dipping sauce. Serve with the grated daikon radish. Replenish the broth as needed. When the food has been eaten, add the noodles to the broth, cook briefly, and then ladle out the soup.

Classic Fonduta

Ingredients

- 1 truffle

- 2½ tablespoons butter

- 1¼ pounds Fontina cheese

- Salt and freshly ground white pepper to taste

- 1¾ cups milk

- 4 egg yolks

- 1 loaf Italian bread, sliced and toasted

- ⅓ cup light cream

Directions

1. Cut the truffle into thin shavings and set aside. Finely dice the Fontina cheese. Place the cheese and the milk in the saucepan. Let the cheese soak for at least 4 hours.

2. Drain the milk from the cheese, reserving 1¼ cups. Heat the reserved milk on low heat, without bringing to a boil. Place the warmed milk and the soaked cheese in a metal bowl on top of a saucepan half-filled with boiling water (or in the top half of a double boiler). Heat over low heat, stirring, until the cheese turns creamy. Whisk in the egg yolks, cream, and butter. Keep whisking until the cheese forms strings. Let it sit for a minute until it just begins to thicken, but not to the point where the egg starts scrambling. Stir in the salt and white pepper.

3. Transfer to a fondue pot and set on the burner. Just before serving, sprinkle the shaved truffle slices over the fondue. Serve with the toasted bread for dipping.

Greek Fondue with Alcohol

- ¾ pound Emmenthal cheese
- 1 tablespoon lemon juice
- ½ pound feta cheese
- 1½ tablespoons cornstarch
- 1 garlic clove
- Marinated Tomatoes
- 1¼ cups plus 2 tablespoons dry white wine
- Toasted Flatbread

Directions

1. Finely dice the cheeses. Smash the garlic clove, peel, and cut in half.

2. Rub the garlic around the inside of a medium saucepan. Discard. Add 1¼ cups wine to the pan and cook on medium-low heat. Don't allow the wine to boil.

3. When the wine is warm, stir in the lemon juice. Add the cheese, a handful at a time. Stir the cheese continually in a sideways figure eight pattern. Wait until the cheese is completely melted before adding more. Don't allow the fondue mixture to boil.

4. Dissolve the cornstarch in the remaining 2 tablespoons of wine. When the cheese is melted, stir in the cornstarch-and-wine mixture. Turn up the heat until the cheese is just bubbling and starting to thicken. Transfer to a fondue pot and set on the burner. Serve with the Marinated Tomatoes as a side dish and the flatbread for dipping.

Vietnamese Beef Hot Pot

Ingredients

- 16 ounces tenderloin beef or any tender cut
- 8 ounces rice vermicelli noodles
- 1 cup mung bean sprouts

- 1 teaspoon freshly ground black pepper

- 1 jar pickled onions

- 1 bunch fresh mint leaves

- 2 teaspoons sugar

- $\frac{1}{3}$ cup nuoc mam fish sauce

- 1 cucumber

- ½ cup Asian hoisin sauce

- 3 green onions

- Lemon-Soy Dressing

- 1 head lettuce

- ¼ cup crushed peanuts

- 1 bunch fresh coriander

- Vietnamese Beef Broth (), as needed

- 24 rice paper wrappers

Directions

1. Cut the beef into paper-thin slices, or have it cut at the butcher shop. Sprinkle lightly with the black pepper and sugar. Refrigerate until needed.

2. Wash or rinse all the vegetables and drain thoroughly. Peel the cucumber and cut lengthwise into thin slices no more than 2 inches long. Cut the green onions into 2-inch slices. Break the lettuce into individual leaves. Chop the coriander leaves.

3. Dip the rice paper wrappers briefly in warm water to dampen. Rinse the rice vermicelli and cover with warm water for 15 minutes to soften. Drain thoroughly. Place the lettuce, cucumber, mung bean sprouts, pickled onions, coriander, and mint leaves on a large serving platter, with the rice paper wrappers in the middle. Set out the nuoc mam fish sauce, hoisin sauce, Lemon-Soy Dressing, and crushed peanuts for dipping.

4. Heat the broth on the stove and bring to a boil. Add the green onions and softened noodles. Transfer enough broth to fill the fondue pot about ⅔ full. Set the fondue pot on the burner, with enough heat to keep the broth simmering throughout the meal.

5. Encourage guests to take a rice paper wrapper and add a selection of vegetables. Use dipping forks to spear the beef. Cook the beef in the hot broth and place on top of the vegetables lying on the wrapper. Roll up the wrapper and dip into the dipping sauces. At the end of the meal, ladle out the broth with the noodles.

Welsh Rarebit

Ingredients

- 1 loaf bread

- 1½ cups beer or ale

- 1 pound aged Cheddar cheese

- ½ teaspoon cayenne pepper

- 2 tablespoons butter or margarine

- 1 teaspoon dry mustard

- Salt and pepper to taste

Directions

1. Toast the bread and cut into cubes. Finely dice the Cheddar cheese.

2. Melt the butter in a saucepan on medium-low heat. Add the beer and warm, making sure it doesn't boil. When the beer is warm, add the cheese, a handful at a time. Stir the cheese continually in a sideways figure eight pattern. Wait until the cheese is completely melted before adding more. Don't allow the fondue mixture to come to a boil.

3. When the cheese is melted, turn up the heat until it is just bubbling and starting to thicken. Stir in the cayenne, dry mustard, and salt and pepper. Transfer to a fondue pot and set on the burner. Serve with the toasted bread cubes for dipping.

Serves 3–4 For an added touch, pour a small amount of beer around the edges of the toast before dipping into the cheese.

Saucy French Fondue

Ingredients

- ¾ pound Emmenthal cheese

- French Pistou with Cheese

- ¼ pound Gruyère cheese

- 1½ tablespoons flour

- 1 baguette, cut into cubes

- 1½ cups dry white wine

- 2 teaspoons lemon juice

Directions

1. Finely dice the cheeses and toss with the flour.

2. Warm the wine in a saucepan on medium-low heat. Don't allow the wine to boil. Remove ¼ cup of the wine and keep warm on low heat in a separate saucepan.

3. When the wine is warm, stir in the lemon juice. Add the cheese, a handful at a time. Stir the cheese continually in a sideways figure eight pattern. Wait until the cheese is completely melted before adding more. Don't allow the fondue mixture to boil.

4. When the cheese is melted, turn up the heat until it is just bubbling and starting to thicken. Stir in the pistou. Add the remaining ¼ cup of wine if necessary. Transfer to a fondue pot and set on the burner. Use dipping forks to dip the bread cubes into the cheese.

Italian Pesto Fondue with Ham

Ingredients

- 8 ounces cooked ham

- Italian Pesto with Basil and Pine Nuts

- 8 ounces prosciutto

- 8 ounces fresh small mushrooms

- 1 loaf Italian bread, cubed, or Bruschetta Fondue Cubes with Vegetables

- 2 red bell peppers

- 4–6 cups olive oil, or as needed

Directions

1. Roll up the ham and prosciutto and cut into bite-sized pieces. Wipe the mushrooms with a damp cloth. Cut the mushrooms in half. Remove the seeds and stems from the red peppers, and cut the peppers into cubes.

2. Add the oil to the fondue pot, making sure it is not more than half full. Heat the pot on a stove element over medium-high heat. When the oil is hot, move the fondue pot to the table and set up the burner.

3. Use dipping forks to spear the rolled-up slices of ham and prosciutto and the vegetables. Cook in the hot oil. Serve with the pesto and the Italian bread or bruschetta cubes.

Italian Pesto Fondue with Cheese

Ingredients

- ¼ pound Fontina cheese

- 1 cup dry white wine

- ½ pound Gruyère cheese

- 2 teaspoons lemon juice

- 1 tablespoon cornstarch

- ½ cup Italian Pesto with Basil and Pine Nuts

- ½ teaspoon dried oregano

- 1 garlic clove, peeled and halved

- 1 package soft breadsticks

Directions

1. Finely dice the Fontina and Gruyère. Mix the cornstarch with the oregano. Toss the cheese with the cornstarch mixture.

2. Rub the garlic around the inside of a medium saucepan. Discard. Add the wine to the saucepan and warm on medium-low heat. Don't allow the wine to boil. Remove ¼ cup of the wine and keep warm on low heat in a separate saucepan.

3. When the wine is warm, stir in the lemon juice. Add the cheese, a handful at a time. Stir the cheese continually in a sideways figure eight pattern. Wait until the cheese is completely melted before adding more. Don't allow the fondue mixture to boil.

4. When the cheese is melted, turn up the heat until it is just bubbling and starting to thicken. Stir in the pesto. Add the remaining ¼ cup of wine if necessary. Transfer to a fondue pot and set on the burner. Serve with the soft breadsticks for dipping.

Mild Bagna Cauda

Ingredients

- ½ cup mushroom caps
- 4 garlic cloves
- 1 small head broccoli
- 1 white truffle
- 1 small head cauliflower
- ½ cup olive oil
- 2 red peppers
- 4 tablespoons butter
- 1 zucchini
- 4 tablespoons light or heavy cream
- 2 stalks celery
- 4 ounces anchovies
- Basic Bruschetta

Directions

1. Wipe the mushrooms clean with a damp cloth and wash the other vegetables. Blanch the broccoli and cauliflower briefly in boiling water and drain thoroughly. Cut the vegetables into bite-sized pieces.

2. Rinse the anchovies, drain, and separate. Smash and peel the garlic cloves, leaving the cloves whole. Thinly slice the truffle.

3. Heat the olive oil and butter in a frying pan over low heat. Add the garlic cloves. Cook over very low heat for 10 minutes, and then add the anchovies. Continue to cook on low heat, gently mashing the anchovies and mixing together with the garlic. Add the cream.

4. Transfer the Bagna Cauda to a fondue pot and set on the burner. Serve with the vegetables for dipping, or with your own favorite combination of mixed vegetables. Eat with the bruschetta.

Beef and Peppers with Clarified Butter

Ingredients

- 1½ pounds beef tenderloin
- 10 ounces clarified butter
- 2 red bell peppers
- 1 cup vegetable oil
- 1 green bell pepper
- Horseradish Cream
- 10 fresh small mushrooms
- Mint and Cilantro Chutney
- 1 red onion
- 2 tablespoons butter or margarine

Directions

1. Cut the beef into cubes. Wash the red and green peppers and dry thoroughly. Cut in half, remove the seeds, and cut into cubes. Wipe the mushrooms clean with a damp cloth. Dry and cut in half. Peel and chop the onion.

2. Heat the 2 tablespoons of butter in a pan. Add the chopped onion, and sauté until it is soft and translucent. Set aside.

3. Add the clarified butter and the oil to the fondue pot. Heat the pot on a stove element over medium-high heat.

4. When the oil is hot, move the fondue pot to the table, set on the burner, and maintain the heat. Use dipping forks to spear the beef and vegetables. Cook the mushroom slices briefly in the hot oil until golden, and the beef until it is cooked through. Cook the peppers very briefly. Drain on paper towels or a tempura rack if desired. Serve with the horseradish cream for dipping. Eat with the sautéed onion and chutney.

Rib-Sticking Meat and Potatoes Hot Pot

Ingredients

- Honey Mustard Sauce

- 6 ounces spinach leaves

- 4 garlic cloves

- 2 pounds beef sirloin steak

- Simple Beef Broth

- 4 small potatoes

- Béarnaise Sauce

- 2 carrots

- Aioli

Directions

1. Warm the honey mustard sauce over low heat. Cut the meat into thin strips.

2. Wash the potatoes and cook in boiling salted water until tender but not soft. Wash the carrots, peel, and cut lengthwise into thin slices. Blanch briefly in boiling water and drain thoroughly. Wash the spinach leaves and drain thoroughly. Smash and peel the garlic cloves.

3. Heat the broth with the garlic cloves on the stove and bring to a boil. Add the spinach and bring to a boil again. Transfer enough broth to fill the fondue pot about ⅔ full. Set the fondue pot on the burner, with enough heat to keep the broth simmering throughout the meal. (Keep the remaining broth warm on the stove to use as needed.)

4. Ladle a small portion of the broth with spinach into the soup bowls. Invite guests to use chopsticks or dipping forks to cook the beef and remaining vegetables in the hot pot. Dip the cooked beef in the dipping sauces, or enjoy with the bowls of broth.

Sesame Beef Appetizer

Ingredients

- 1 cup sesame seeds

- 4½ cups oil, or as needed

- 10 ounces beef round

- 5 tablespoons sesame seed oil

- ¼ cup Quick and Easy Teriyaki Marinade

Directions

1. Toast the sesame seeds by spreading out on a frying pan and cooking at low heat until they brown. Cool.

2. Cut the beef into thin slices approximately 3 inches long and ½ inch wide. Place in a shallow glass dish. Toss the meat with the marinade. Refrigerate and marinate the meat for 1 hour. Remove any excess marinade and place the meat on a serving platter.

3. Add the oil to the fondue pot, making sure it is not more than half full. Heat the pot on a stove element over medium-high heat.

4. When the oil is hot, move the fondue pot to the table and set up the burner. Invite guests to roll up the beef slices and spear them with a dipping fork or a metal skewer with a wooden handle. Cook in the hot oil briefly until the meat is cooked. Dip into the sesame oil and the toasted sesame seeds.

Classic Bacchus Fondue

Ingredients

- 2 pounds beef rib steak

- 4 cups dry red wine, or as needed

- 2 shallots

- Basic Red Wine Marinade

- Béarnaise Sauce

- Curried Yogurt

- ¾ pound fresh small mushrooms

- Horseradish with Sour Cream

- 2 green onions

Directions

1. Cut the beef into thin strips. Peel and chop the shallots. Place the meat and the shallots in a shallow glass dish and pour the marinade over. Refrigerate and marinate the beef for 1 hour. Remove any excess marinade.

2. Wipe the mushrooms with a damp cloth. Remove the stems. Chop the green onions.

3. Heat the wine on the stove or in the fondue pot. Make sure not to fill the pot more than ⅔

full. Stir in the green onions. Keep the wine simmering throughout the meal.

4. Use dipping forks to spear the beef strips and mushroom caps. Cook in the wine for 3 to 4 minutes until cooked through. Serve with the sauces for dipping.

Beef Carpaccio

Ingredients

- 8 ounces beef tenderloin, sliced paper thin
- ¼ cup lemon juice
- 2 tablespoons freshly cracked black pepper
- 4 plum tomatoes, fresh or canned
- Pesto Mayonnaise
- 2 tablespoons extra-virgin olive oil
- 1 jar capers

Directions

1. Keep the beef chilled until ready to serve. Wash the tomatoes, pat dry, and cut into wedges.

2. Place the beef between pieces of plastic wrap lightly oiled with the olive oil. Pound with a mallet to thin the beef even further. Remove the beef from the wrap and brush with the lemon juice. Sprinkle with the freshly cracked black pepper.

3. Cut the beef into medium-sized pieces that can be comfortably skewered with a dipping fork. Place on a large serving platter. Garnish with the tomato wedges.

4. Place the Pesto Mayonnaise in a cheese or dessert fondue bowl in the middle of the table. Invite guests to skewer the beef slices and dip them into the Pesto Mayonnaise. Serve with the capers.

Basic Marinated Chicken Fondue

Ingredients

- Mediterranean Chicken Marinade
- 5 cups oil, or as needed
- 1 pound skinless, boneless chicken breasts

Directions

1. Let the marinade sit for 1 hour before coating chicken.

2. Wash the chicken breasts and pat dry. Cut into 1-inch cubes. Place in a glass dish. Pour the marinade over the chicken, cover, and refrigerate for 1 hour.

3. Drain the marinade from the chicken and pat dry with paper towels.

4. Add the oil to the fondue pot, making sure it is not more than half full. Heat the pot on a stove element over medium-high heat.

5. When the oil is hot, move the fondue pot to the table and set up the burner. Skewer the chicken cubes so that the skewer goes right through the meat. Cook the chicken cubes in the hot oil for 2 to 3 minutes, until they are browned and cooked through.

Marinated Chicken Wings

Ingredients

- 2 pounds chicken wings
- 4–5 cups oil, or as needed
- ⅔ cup Mediterranean Chicken Marinade
-

1. Rinse the chicken wings and pat dry. Cut through the wings at the joints.

2. Place the wings in a shallow glass dish and brush with the marinade on both sides. Refrigerate the chicken and marinate for 1 hour. Pat dry and remove any excess marinade.

3. Add the oil to the fondue pot, making sure it is not more than half full. Heat the pot on a stove element over medium-high heat.

4. When the oil is hot, move the fondue pot to the table and set up the burner. Use dipping forks or metal skewers to skewer the chicken wings. Cook in the hot oil until the wings are browned and cooked through.

Elegant Butterflied Shrimp in Liqueur

Ingredients

- 4 garlic cloves
- 1 cup cream
- 1 pound fresh asparagus spears

- 1 cup orange liqueur (such as Grand Marnier)

- 24 large raw shrimp, peeled and deveined, tails on

- ½ teaspoon nutmeg

- ½ cup fresh baby dill

- 2 tablespoons butter

- ¼ cup cayenne pepper

Directions

1. Smash and peel the garlic. Trim the ends off the asparagus, cook in boiling salted water until tender, and drain thoroughly. Cut into 2-inch pieces.

2. Rinse the shrimp in cold water and pat dry with paper towels. To butterfly the shrimp, make an incision lengthwise down the back. Cut down as deeply as possible without cutting right through the shrimp. Halfway down the back, make two parallel cuts on the left and right of the incision. Flatten down the four quarters as much as possible. Place the butterflied shrimp on a large serving platter with the asparagus pieces.

3. In a medium saucepan, melt the butter on low heat. Add the garlic and cook on low heat in the melting butter for 2 to 3 minutes. Add the cream. Carefully add the orange liqueur to the warmed cream. Stir in the nutmeg, baby dill, and the cayenne pepper.

4. Transfer the dish to a fondue pot and set on the burner at the table. Use dipping forks to spear the shrimp and cook in the fondue until they change color. Eat with the asparagus (if desired, the asparagus can be dipped briefly into the fondue).

Fish in White Sauce

Ingredients

- 2 pounds fresh fish fillets (such as sole)

- 1 ⅓ cups White Sauce for Seafood

- Lemony Ginger Marinade

- 4 cups oil, or as needed

Directions

1. Pat the fish dry and cut into bite-sized cubes. Place the fish in a shallow glass dish. Pour the

marinade over and marinate the fish for 15 minutes. Remove any excess marinade. Prepare the white sauce and keep warm over low heat.

2. Add the oil to the fondue pot, making sure it is not more than half full. Heat the pot on a stove element over medium-high heat. When the oil is hot, move the fondue pot to the table and set up the burner.

3. Use dipping forks to spear the fish cubes and cook very briefly (about 15 seconds) in the hot oil. Dip into the white sauce.

Tempura Oysters

Ingredients

- 12 fresh oysters

- 4 cups oil, or as needed

- Tempura Batter

Directions

1. Shuck the oysters, rinse in warm water, and drain thoroughly. Prepare the batter.

2. Add the oil to the fondue pot, making sure it is not more than half full. Heat the pot on a stove element over medium-high heat. When the oil is hot, move the fondue pot to the table and set up the burner. Use dipping forks to spear the oysters and dip into the batter. Cook in the hot oil until golden brown. Drain on paper towels if desired.

Chinese-Style Butterfly Shrimp

Ingredients

- 1 pound large shrimp

- ⅔ cup bread crumbs

- 2 teaspoons Chinese cooking wine

- 4 cups oil, or as needed

- ½ teaspoon freshly ground white pepper

- ½ teaspoon sugar

- 2 eggs

- ½ teaspoon freshly ground black pepper
- 1 teaspoon five-spice powder

Directions

1. Peel the shrimp but leave the tail on. Cut a slit along the back, being careful not to cut through. Open the two cut halves to form a butterfly shape. If there is a black sand vein, remove it.

2. Rinse the shrimp in cold water and pat dry. Marinate in the cooking wine and sugar for 15 minutes.

3. Lightly beat the eggs. In a separate bowl, mix the five-spice powder with the bread crumbs.

4. Add the oil to the fondue pot, making sure it is not more than half full. Heat the pot on a stove element over medium-high heat.

5. When the oil is hot, move the fondue pot to the table and set up the burner. Grab the shrimp by the tail and dip into the egg, then coat with the bread crumbs. Spear the shrimp with the dipping fork and cook in the hot oil until golden brown. Drain on paper towels if desired. Dip lightly into the black or white pepper.

Breaded Red Snapper

Ingredients

- 8 slices fresh bread (to make 2 cups crumbs)
- 2 eggs
- ½ medium yellow onion
- 4 tablespoons fresh baby dill leaves, chopped
- 4½ cups oil, or as needed
- Seafood Cocktail Sauce
- ⅛ teaspoon each salt and pepper
- Quick and Easy Tartar Sauce
- 1 pound fresh red snapper fillets
- ¼ cup Quick and Easy Teriyaki Marinade

Directions

1. Cut the crusts off the bread and process in the food processor. Add the dill leaves and salt and pepper and process again.

2. Pat the red snapper fillets dry and cut into bite-sized cubes. Place the fish in a shallow glass dish. Pour the marinade over and marinate the fish for 15 minutes. Remove any excess marinade.

3. Lightly beat the eggs and place in a small bowl at the table, alongside the bread crumbs. Peel and chop the onion.

4. Add the oil to the fondue pot, making sure it is not more than half full. Heat the pot on a stove element over medium-high heat. When the oil is hot, move the fondue pot to the table and set up the burner.

5. Place the chopped onion in a dipping basket in the oil. Fry briefly and then remove. Use dipping forks to spear the fish cubes. Dip into the egg wash and coat with the bread crumbs. Fry in the hot oil until the bread crumbs turn golden brown (about 30 seconds). Dip into the cocktail or tartar sauce. Eat with the fried onion.

Le Grand Aioli

Ingredients

- 1 pound salted cod
- 1 pound green beans
- 4 medium beets
- 1 pound mussels
- 4 red-skinned potatoes
- 8 hard-boiled eggs
- 1 cup baby carrots
- Aioli

Directions

1. The day before serving the meal, place the salted cod in cold water. Soak for 24 hours, changing the water several times.

2. One hour before the meal is to be served, preheat the oven to 350°F. Wrap the beets in foil

and bake for 1 hour, or until the beets are tender.

3. Blanch the remaining vegetables in boiling salted water. Begin with the potatoes. When they are nearly tender, add the carrots and green beans. Peel and julienne the carrots. Cut the potatoes into bite-sized chunks.

4. Poach the cod in boiling water for 15 minutes. Drain thoroughly and break into pieces. Rinse the mussels under cold water, scrubbing the shells with a stiff brush. Poach in boiling water for 4 to 5 minutes. Drain thoroughly. Peel the hard-boiled eggs and cut into halves.

5. To serve, place the Aioli in a cheese fondue serving dish. Arrange the vegetables on a serving platter. Place the hard-boiled eggs on top. Serve the cod and mussels on another platter. Use dipping forks to spear the vegetables and seafood and dip into the aioli.

Poached Mussels and Prawns in Wine

Ingredients

- 12 mussels

- ¼ cup cream

- 2 teaspoons salt

- ¼ teaspoon pepper

- 12 prawns, peeled and deveined

- 2 tablespoons fresh parsley, chopped

- 2 garlic cloves

- Quick and Easy Blender Hollandaise Sauce

- ¼ yellow onion

- 2 tablespoons olive oil

- Seafood Cocktail Sauce

- 1 cup dry white wine

- 1 cup clam juice

Directions

1. Under cold running water, scrub the mussels with a stiff brush to remove any dirt. Soak the mussels in cold water for 5 minutes. Rinse and repeat. Steam the mussels in boiling water for

5 minutes until they open. Rinse and remove from the shells. Throw out any mussels that don't open. Dissolve the salt in 3 cups of warm water. Rinse the prawns in the warm water for 5 minutes and pat dry.

2. Smash the garlic cloves, peel, and chop. Peel and chop the onion. Heat the olive oil on low heat in a fondue pot or a medium saucepan. Add the onion and cook briefly. Add the chopped garlic cloves and cook on low heat until the onion is soft.

3. Turn up the heat to medium-low and add the wine. Warm briefly and add the clam juice. Add the cream. Stir in the pepper and chopped parsley.

4. Transfer the broth to the fondue pot if necessary; set the fondue pot on the table and set up the burner. Place the mussels and prawns on a serving platter. Use dipping forks to spear the seafood and cook in the hot broth. Serve with the sauces for dipping.

Five Flavor Fish Stew

Ingredients

- ¾ pound large shrimp

- 1 shallot

- 1 pound light fish fillets (such as cod)

- 2 tablespoons olive oil

- 1 cup white wine

- 4 large white potatoes

- 4 cups Fish Broth

- ¾ pound asparagus spears

- Speedy Garlic Mayonnaise

- 2 celery stalks

- 1 garlic clove

- ½ cup five-spice powder

Directions

1. Peel and devein the shrimp, leaving the tails on. Rinse the shrimp in cold water, drain, and pat dry. Rinse the fish, pat dry, and cut into bite-sized pieces.

2. Cook the potatoes in boiling water until they can be pierced easily with a fork but are not overly tender. Cool and cut into chunks. Blanch the asparagus spears briefly in boiling water. Drain thoroughly. Cut the spears into 1-inch pieces. Cut the celery stalks diagonally into 1-inch slices. Smash, peel, and chop the garlic clove. Chop the shallot.

3. Heat the olive oil on low heat in a fondue pot or a medium saucepan. Add the shallot and cook briefly on low heat. Add the garlic clove. Turn up the heat to medium-low and add the wine and the broth. Bring to a boil. Transfer the broth to the fondue pot if necessary; set the fondue pot on the table and set up the burner. Set the temperature high enough to keep the broth simmering throughout the meal.

4. Place the shrimp, fish, potatoes, celery, and asparagus on serving platters. Use dipping forks to spear the seafood and asparagus and dip into the hot broth. (The potatoes and celery can be dipped into the broth or eaten as is.) Serve with the mayonnaise and five-spice powder for dipping.

Deep-Fried Mussels

Ingredients

- 1 pound mussels (about 16)
- Seafood Cocktail Sauce
- $1/3$ cup flour
- Tempura Batter
- Lemon-Soy Dressing
- 4 cups oil, or as needed

Directions

1. Under cold running water, scrub the mussels with a stiff brush to remove any dirt. Soak the mussels in cold water for 5 minutes. Rinse and repeat. Steam the mussels in boiling water for 5 minutes until they open. Rinse and remove from the shells. Throw out any mussels that don't open.

2. Dry the mussels thoroughly. Lightly dust with flour and set on a serving platter. Prepare the batter.

3. Add the oil to the fondue pot, making sure it is not more than half full. Heat the pot on a

stove element over medium-high heat. When the oil is hot, move the fondue pot to the table and set up the burner. Keep the oil hot throughout the meal.

4. Spear the mussels with a skewer or dipping fork and coat with the batter. Cook in the hot oil until the batter turns golden brown. Serve with the sauces for dipping.

Cod in Herbed Batter

Ingredients

- 2 pounds frozen cod fillets

- 5 cups oil, or as needed

- 2 zucchini

- Herbed Seafood Batter

- 2 tomatoes

- 1 fresh lemon

- Seafood Cocktail Sauce

- 1 16-ounce can artichokes

- 2 eggs

- Quick and Easy Tartar Sauce

- 1 teaspoon salt

- 1 teaspoon pepper

- Lemon-Soy Dressing

Directions

1. Thaw the cod fillets, dry, and cut into bite-sized pieces. Wash the zucchini, peel, and slice diagonally. Wash the tomatoes. Cut the tomatoes and lemon into wedges. Drain the artichokes and dry.

2. Lightly beat the eggs. Stir in the salt and pepper.

3. Add the oil to the fondue pot, making sure it is not more than half full. Heat the pot on a stove element over medium-high heat. When the oil is hot, move the fondue pot to the table and set up the burner. Keep the oil hot throughout the meal.

4. Use a wooden skewer or dipping fork to spear the fish pieces. Dip into the beaten egg and

coat with the batter. Cook in the hot oil until the batter turns golden brown. Spear the artichokes and cook briefly. Serve with the lemon wedges and the sauces for dipping. Eat with the tomatoes and zucchini.

Fish and Chips

Ingredients

- 4 large potatoes

- Quick and Easy Tartar Sauce

- 1½ pounds frozen fish sticks

- 4½ cups oil, or as needed

- Seafood Cocktail Sauce

Directions

1. Boil the potatoes for about 15 minutes on medium-low heat, until they can be pierced with a fork but are not too soft. Drain thoroughly, and cut lengthwise into pieces approximately ¾ inch thick. Place the potatoes and fish sticks on a serving platter.

2. Add the oil to the fondue pot, making sure it is not more than half full. Heat the pot on a stove element over medium-high heat. When the oil is hot, move the fondue pot to the table and set up the burner.

3. On a skewer, place 2 fish sticks and 2 potato slices, alternating. Lay the skewer crosswise in the hot oil so that both the fish sticks and the potatoes cook evenly. If desired, drain on paper towels after cooking. Serve with the sauces for dipping.

Butterfly Prawns Dipped in Lemon Pepper

Ingredients

- 2 garlic cloves

- 4 cups oil, or as needed

- 2 lemons

- 3 tablespoons lemon pepper

- 24 large prawns, raw or cooked

Directions

1. Smash and peel the garlic cloves. Cut the lemons into wedges.

2. Peel the prawns but leave the tail on. Cut a slit along the back, being careful not to cut through. Open the two cut halves to form a butterfly shape. If there is a black sand vein, remove it. Rinse the prawns in cold water and pat dry.

3. Add the oil to the fondue pot, making sure it is not more than half full. Heat the pot on a stove element over medium-high heat. When the oil is hot, add the garlic cloves. Brown and then remove them from the pot. Move the fondue pot to the table and set up the burner.

4. Place the butterflied prawns on a serving plate, with the lemon wedges as a garnish. Use dipping forks to spear the prawns and cook in the hot oil until golden brown. Drain on paper towels if desired. Dip into the lemon pepper.

Teriyaki Fish Fry

Ingredients

- 1 pound fresh red snapper fillets

- 2 shallots

- 3 tablespoons olive oil

- ¾ pound fresh flounder fillets

- 2 fresh lemons

- 2 portions Quick and Easy Teriyaki Marinade

- 4½ cups oil, or as needed

- Seafood Cocktail Sauce

- 6 potatoes

- 2 green bell peppers

- Homemade Tartar Sauce

- 1 red onion

Directions

1. Pat the fish fillets dry and cut into pieces roughly 2 inches long and 1 inch wide. Place the fish in shallow glass dishes, keeping the snapper and flounder separate. Set 1 portion of the Quick and Easy Teriyaki Marinade aside to serve as a dipping sauce. Pour just over half of

the remaining portion of the marinade over the red snapper, and the rest over the flounder. Marinate the fish for 15 minutes. Remove any excess marinade.

2. Boil the potatoes on medium-low heat for about 15 minutes, until they can be pierced with a fork but are not too soft. Drain thoroughly. Wash the green peppers, drain thoroughly, and cut into bite-sized cubes. Peel and chop the onion and shallots.

3. Heat the olive oil in a frying pan. Sauté the onion and shallots until soft. Keep warm. Cut the lemons into wedges.

4. Add the oil to the fondue pot, making sure it is not more than half full. Heat the pot on a stove element over medium-high heat. When the oil is hot, move the fondue pot to the table and set up the burner. Keep the oil hot throughout the meal.

5. Spear the fish on wooden skewers, with the ends sticking through. Cook the fish and the green bell peppers briefly in the hot oil. Serve with the lemon wedges and the sauces and teriyaki marinade for dipping. Eat with the potatoes and sautéed onion and shallots.

Cheesy Tomato Fondue

Ingredients

- ½ pound Swiss Emmenthal cheese
- 1 cup dry white wine
- 2 teaspoons lemon juice
- ½ pound Gruyère cheese
- 1½ tablespoons cornstarch
- 4 medium tomatoes
- 2 tablespoons water
- ½ teaspoon thyme
- Bruschetta Fondue Cubes with Vegetables
- ¼ teaspoon oregano
- Salt and pepper to taste
- 1 garlic clove, smashed, peeled, and cut in half

Directions

1. Preheat the oven to 350°F. Finely dice the cheese. Wash the tomatoes, dry, and cut off the stems. Peel and cut each tomato into 8 equal slices.

2. Mix the tomato slices with the thyme, oregano, and salt and pepper. Lay the slices flat on a baking tray and bake for approximately 25 minutes, making sure that the bottoms of the tomatoes don't burn.

3. While the tomatoes are baking, prepare the cheese fondue. Rub the garlic around the inside of a medium saucepan. Discard. Add the wine to the pan and cook on low heat. Don't allow the wine to boil.

4. When the wine is warm, stir in the lemon juice. Add the cheese, a handful at a time. Stir the cheese continually in a sideways figure eight pattern. Wait until the cheese is completely melted before adding more. Don't allow the fondue mixture to boil.

5. When the cheese is melted, dissolve the cornstarch in the water and add to the cheese. Turn up the heat until it is just bubbling and starting to thicken. Transfer to a fondue pot and set on the burner. Serve with the baked tomato slices and bruschetta cubes for dipping.

Korean Bulgogi Hot Pot

Ingredients

- 1½ pounds beef flank steak

- 1 cucumber

- 2 tablespoons soy sauce

- 2 green onions

- 1½ teaspoons sugar

- 1 8-ounce can baby corn

- 1½ tablespoons rice vinegar

- 1 bunch cilantro sprigs

- 1½ teaspoons sesame oil

- 4 cups cooked rice

- ½ large daikon radish

- 6 cups Simple Beef Broth

- 4 large carrots

Directions

1. Cut the beef into paper-thin slices. Combine the soy sauce, sugar, rice vinegar, and sesame oil in a small bowl. Add the beef and marinate for at least 30 minutes.

2. Wash all the vegetables and drain. Peel the daikon radish. Cut in half and then into slices about 2½ inches long. Do the same with the carrots. Peel and slice the cucumber on the diagonal into slices about 1 inch thick. Chop the green onions. Rinse the baby corn in warm water and drain.

3. Place the marinated beef and vegetables on separate serving platters. Garnish the vegetables with the cilantro. Serve each guest an individual bowl half-filled with cooked rice.

4. Heat the broth on the stove, and bring to a boil. Add the meat and vegetables and bring to a boil again. Transfer enough broth to fill the fondue pot about ⅔ full. Set the fondue pot on the burner, with enough heat to keep the broth simmering throughout the meal. (Keep the remaining broth warm on the stove to use as needed.)

5. At the table, allow the hot pot to cook for another 5 minutes. Ladle a small portion of the broth with meat and vegetables into the soup bowls over rice. Invite guests to use chopsticks to eat the food.

Classic Tiramisu

Ingredients

- 4 egg yolks

- 2 teaspoons powdered hot chocolate

- 4 tablespoons sugar

- 4 ounces semisweet chocolate

- 1 tablespoon cornstarch

- 1 pound mascarpone cheese

- 24 ladyfingers

- 8 tablespoons Marsala wine

- 2 tablespoons espresso or strong hot coffee

Directions

1. Whisk the egg yolks with the sugar and set aside. Grate the chocolate and set aside.

2. Whisk the mascarpone with 6 tablespoons Marsala wine. Combine with 1 tablespoon of the espresso in a metal bowl and place on top of a saucepan half-filled with simmering water. Melt the mixture on low to medium-low heat, stirring frequently and making sure that it doesn't boil.

3. When the mascarpone has melted and has a texture close to pudding, stir in the hot chocolate. Dissolve the cornstarch in 2 tablespoons Marsala wine and stir into the fondue. Whisk in the egg yolks to thicken.

4. Transfer the fondue mixture to the fondue pot and set on the burner. Keep warm on low heat. Just before serving, sprinkle with the grated chocolate. Brush the ladyfingers with the remainder of the coffee and serve with the fondue for dipping.

Toblerone Fondue with Orange Liqueur

Ingredients

*   1 pound fresh strawberries
*   ⅔ cup half-and-half or light cream
*   2 tablespoons freshly squeezed orange juice
*   4 teaspoons Grand Marnier liqueur
*   4 3.5-ounce (100-gram) Toblerone milk chocolate bars

Directions

1. Wash and drain the strawberries on paper towels. Remove the hulls. Lightly sprinkle the orange juice over the drained strawberries.

2. Break the Toblerone bars into pieces. Combine the cream and Toblerone pieces in a metal bowl and place on top of a saucepan half-filled with simmering water. Melt the mixture on low to medium-low heat, stirring frequently. Make sure that it doesn't boil.

3. Carefully add the Grand Marnier to the heated chocolate, 1 teaspoon at a time. Transfer the chocolate mixture into the fondue pot and set on the burner.

4. Keep warm on low heat. Use dipping forks to dip the strawberries into the chocolate fondue.

Basic Chocolate Fondue

Ingredients

- 8 ounces semisweet chocolate
- 2 pounds fresh fruit (or 1 pound each fresh fruit and cake)
- 1 cup whipping cream
- 1 tablespoon liqueur, optional

Directions

1. Break the chocolate into pieces. Combine the whipping cream and chocolate in a metal bowl and place on top of a saucepan half-filled with simmering water. Melt the mixture on low to medium-low heat, stirring frequently. Make sure that it doesn't boil.

2. When the chocolate is melted, stir in the liqueur. Transfer the chocolate mixture into the fondue pot and set on the burner. Keep warm on low heat. Use dipping forks to dip the fruit and/or cake into the fondue.

Basic Chocolate Chip Fondue for Four

Ingredients

- 1¾ cups chocolate chips
- 1 tablespoon liqueur, optional
- ⅓ cup plus 2 tablespoons light cream
- 4 cups fresh fruit for dipping

Directions

1. Combine the chocolate chips and cream in a metal bowl and place on top of a saucepan half-filled with simmering water. Melt the chocolate on low to medium-low heat, stirring frequently and making sure that it doesn't boil. Stir in the liqueur.

2. Transfer the fondue mixture to the fondue pot and set on the burner. Keep the fondue warm on low heat. Serve with fresh fruit for dipping.

Instant Mocha

Ingredients

- 8 ounces semisweet chocolate

- 2 medium oranges, peeled and sliced

- ¾ cup coffee cream

- ¼ teaspoon nutmeg

- Biscuits or biscotti

- 1 can pineapple chunks, drained

Directions

1. Break the semisweet chocolate into pieces. Combine the coffee cream and chocolate in a metal bowl and place over a saucepan half-filled with simmering water. Melt the chocolate on low to medium-low heat, stirring constantly and not allowing the mixture to boil.

2. When the chocolate is melted, transfer the fondue mixture to the fondue pot and set on the burner. Keep the fondue warm on low heat. Stir in the nutmeg.

3. Serve the fondue with pineapple chunks, sliced oranges, and biscuits or fruit-flavored biscotti for dipping.

Quick and Easy Butterscotch Fondue

Ingredients

- 4 bananas

- 3 tablespoons powdered hot chocolate

- 3 cups canned pear slices

- ½ cup light cream

- ½ teaspoon vanilla extract

- 1¾ cups butterscotch chips

- 1 tablespoon Kahlua

Directions

1. Peel the bananas and slice diagonally. Drain the pear slices and dry on paper towels.

2. Combine the cream and butterscotch chips in a metal bowl and place on top of a saucepan half-filled with simmering water. Melt on low to medium-low heat, stirring constantly. Do not allow the mixture to boil. When the butterscotch chips are completely melted, stir in the hot chocolate, vanilla extract, and the Kahlua.

3. Transfer the fondue mixture to the fondue pot and set on the burner. Keep the fondue warm on low heat. Serve with the fruit for dipping.

Elegant Chocolate Fondue

Ingredients

- 1 cup light cream
- 2 tablespoons cognac Cake, biscuits, or fruit for dipping
- 4 heaping tablespoons fresh mint leaves, chopped
- 12 ounces semisweet chocolate

Directions

1. In a small saucepan, heat the cream with the mint leaves over low heat for 15–20 minutes, until the mint leaves are tender and the cream almost has a faint greenish color. Strain the cream to remove the mint leaves. Break the chocolate into pieces.

2. Combine the cream and the chocolate in a metal bowl and place over a saucepan half-filled with simmering water. Melt the chocolate on low to medium-low heat, stirring constantly. Do not allow the mixture to boil. Add more cream if necessary.

3. When the chocolate has melted, transfer the fondue mixture to the fondue pot and set on the burner. Keep the fondue warm on low heat. Stir in the cognac. Serve with sponge cake, biscuits, or fresh fruit for dipping. It goes very well with fresh fruit such as apples, pineapples, and bananas, and fruit-flavored biscotti.

Cinnamon Fondue

Ingredients

- 1 pound fresh strawberries
- 1 cup heavy cream
- 8 ounces semisweet chocolate
- 1 teaspoon cinnamon
- 4 ounces unsweetened chocolate

Directions

1. Wash and drain the strawberries on paper towels. Remove the hulls. Break the semisweet and unsweetened chocolate into pieces.

2. Combine the cream and chocolate in a metal bowl and place over a saucepan half-filled with barely simmering water. Melt the chocolate on low to medium-low heat, stirring constantly. Do not let the mixture overheat. Add more cream if necessary.

3. When the chocolate has melted, transfer the fondue mixture to the fondue pot and set on the burner. Keep the fondue warm on low heat. Stir in the cinnamon. Serve with the strawberries for dipping.

Cool Yogurt Fondue

Ingredients

- 6 tablespoons unsweetened coconut flakes

- 2 peaches

- 2 peaches

- 3 teaspoons lime juice

- 3 tablespoons lemon juice

- 3½ tablespoons liquid honey

- 2 bananas

- 2 cups plain yogurt

Directions

1. Stir the coconut flakes, lime juice, and honey into the yogurt. Chill until ready to serve.

2. Wash the peaches and apples and drain thoroughly. Cut into wedges and lightly cover with the lemon juice. Peel the bananas and cut into 1-inch slices.

3. Use a dipping fork to dip the fruit pieces into the chilled yogurt.

Peanut Butter Fondue

Ingredients

- 4 large bananas

- 1 cup milk

- 4 ounces milk chocolate

- Peanut butter cookies, optional

- 1 cup chunky peanut butter

Directions

1. Peel and slice the bananas. Break the chocolate into pieces.

2. Combine the peanut butter, milk, and milk chocolate in a metal bowl and place on top of a saucepan half-filled with simmering water. Melt the chocolate on low to medium-low heat, stirring constantly. Make sure that it doesn't boil.

3. Transfer the fondue mixture to the fondue pot and set on the burner. Keep the fondue warm on low heat. Serve with the bananas and cookies for dipping.

Chocolate Banana Fondue

Ingredients

- ½ cup half-and-half or light cream

- ⅓ cup Sweet Banana Chutney

- 1½ cups semisweet chocolate chips

- ¼ cup crushed peanuts

Directions

1. Combine the cream and semisweet chocolate in a metal bowl and place over a saucepan half-filled with simmering water. Melt the chocolate on low to medium-low heat, stirring continuously and making sure it doesn't boil. When the chocolate is melted, stir in the chutney.

2. Garnish the fondue with the crushed peanuts. Keep the fondue warm on low heat while serving. Serve with sliced apples, sliced bananas, and plain biscuits for dipping.

Three Fruit Medley

Ingredients

- 1 cup fresh strawberries

- 1½ tablespoons brown sugar

- 1 banana

- 1 tablespoon sugar

- 1 cup pineapple chunks

- ½ cup light cream

- 2 tablespoons pineapple juice or water

- 8 ounces semisweet chocolate chips

Directions

1. Wash the strawberries, cut off the stems, and slice. Peel the banana, cut in half lengthwise, and slice. Lay the sliced strawberries and the pineapple chunks flat in a glass serving dish, with the sliced banana in the middle. If using canned pineapple chunks, reserve 2 tablespoons of the juice. Sprinkle the brown sugar over the pineapple chunks and bananas, and the white sugar over the strawberries. Set aside.

2. Combine the cream and chocolate chips in a metal bowl and place over a saucepan half-filled with simmering water. Melt the chocolate chips on low to medium-low heat, stirring constantly and not allowing the mixture to boil. When the chocolate has melted, stir in the reserved pineapple juice or water. Pour over the pineapple chunks, banana slices, and strawberries. Serve warm.

Harvest Apple Fondue

Ingredients

- 3–4 large red apples

- ½ cup cinnamon baking chips

- 1½ cups peanuts

- 2 teaspoons sugar

- ½ cup whipping cream

- ¾ cup semisweet chocolate chips

Directions

1. Core the apples and cut into wedges. Refrigerate until ready to use. Crush the peanuts in a blender or food processor.

2. Combine the cream and chips in a metal bowl and place over a saucepan half-filled with

simmering water. Melt the chips on low to medium-low heat, stirring continuously and making sure the mixture doesn't boil. Stir in the sugar.

3. Transfer the chocolate mixture to a fondue pot over low heat. Remove the apple slices from the refrigerator and set on the table. Set out individual bowls of crushed peanuts for each person. Dip the apple slices in the fondue and then roll in the crushed peanuts.

Mexican Chocolate Fondue with Kahlua and Strawberries

Ingredients

- 1 pound fresh strawberries
- ½ teaspoon nutmeg
- 12 ounces semisweet chocolate
- ¼ teaspoon ground cloves, optional
- ½ cup half-and-half
- ¾ cup evaporated milk
- 1 tablespoon Kahlua, or to taste
- 1 teaspoon ground cinnamon

Directions

1. Wash and drain the strawberries on paper towels. Remove the hulls. Break the chocolate into pieces.

2. Combine the chocolate, half-and-half, and evaporated milk in a metal bowl and place on top of a saucepan half-filled with simmering water. Melt the mixture on low to medium-low heat, making sure that it doesn't boil.

3. When the chocolate is melted, stir in the cinnamon, nutmeg, and ground cloves. Stir in the Kahlua.

4. Transfer the fondue mixture to the fondue pot and set on the burner. Keep the fondue warm on low heat. Serve with the strawberries for dipping.

Spiced Apple Fondue

Ingredients

- 3 medium Spartan apples

- 1¾ cups semisweet chocolate chips

- ¼ cup half-and-half or light cream

- ½ teaspoon cinnamon

- 2 tablespoons apple schnapps

Directions

1. Core the apples and cut into wedges. Combine the cream and chocolate chips in a metal bowl and place over a saucepan half-filled with simmering water. Melt the chips on low to medium-low heat, stirring continuously and making sure the mixture doesn't boil.

2. When the chocolate is melted, transfer the fondue mixture to the fondue pot and set on the burner. Stir in the cinnamon and the apple schnapps. Keep the fondue warm on low heat. Serve with the apple wedges for dipping.

Sweet and Sour Tropical Fondue

Ingredients

- 4 bananas

- 2 tablespoons butter or margarine

- 2 cups tropical dried fruit mix (or another dried fruit mix)

- 2 cups chocolate macaroons

- ¾ cup sour cream

- 2 tablespoons Kahlua

Directions

1. Slice the bananas and set aside with the dried fruit mix.

2. Combine the sour cream, butter, and chocolate macaroons in a metal bowl and place over a saucepan half-filled with simmering water. Heat the mixture on medium-low heat, stirring constantly. Do not let the mixture boil.

3. When the chocolate is melted, stir in the Kahlua. Transfer the mixture to the fondue pot and set on the burner. Keep the fondue warm on low heat. Serve with the bananas and dried fruit

for dipping.

Yin Yang Fondue

Ingredients

- 8 ounces white chocolate
- ¼ cup kirsch
- 8 ounces semisweet chocolate
- 6 cups mixed apple and cantaloupe slices
- ½ cup evaporated milk
- ½ teaspoon cinnamon

Directions

1. Break the chocolate into pieces. Combine the white chocolate, semisweet chocolate, and evaporated milk in a metal bowl and place on top of a saucepan half-filled with simmering water. Melt the mixture on low to medium-low heat, making sure that it doesn't boil.

2. When the chocolate has melted, stir in the cinnamon and the kirsch. Transfer the fondue mixture to the fondue pot and set on the burner. Keep the fondue warm on low heat. Serve with the apple and cantaloupe slices for dipping.

Decadent Chocolate Berry Sauce

Ingredients

- 2 cups mixed frozen strawberries and blueberries
- ⅔ cup whipping cream
- 2 teaspoons lemon juice
- ¼ cup sugar
- Chocolate macaroons and biscuits for dipping, as desired
- 16 ounces milk chocolate

Directions

1. Break up any large frozen strawberries. Simmer the berries in a pot with the sugar for about 10 minutes, until the berries are soft and mushy. Cool and process in a blender or food

processor.

2. Break the chocolate into pieces. Combine the milk chocolate and whipping cream in a metal bowl and place on top of a saucepan half-filled with simmering water. Melt the mixture on low to medium-low heat, making sure that it doesn't boil. Stir in the lemon juice and the processed berries.

3. Transfer the fondue mixture to the fondue pot and set on the burner. Keep the fondue warm on low heat. Serve with the chocolate macaroons or biscuits for dipping.

Hot Yogurt Fondue

Ingredients

- 2 cups plain yogurt

- 1 teaspoon hot chili sauce

- ⅔ cup liquid honey

- 2 tablespoons rum

- 1 teaspoon cinnamon

- 6 cups mixed cantaloupe and kiwifruit or other tropical fruit slices

- 1 teaspoon lime juice

- 1 teaspoon lemon juice

Directions

1. Combine the yogurt, honey, cinnamon, lime juice, lemon juice, and hot chili sauce in a saucepan and cook over medium-low heat until the yogurt has melted. Stir in the rum.

2. Transfer the fondue mixture to the fondue pot and set on the burner. Keep the fondue warm on low heat. Serve with the tropical fruit for dipping.

Two for One Fondue

Ingredients

- ½ Creamy Caramel Fondue for Adults

- 4 tablespoons coconut milk

- 1 tablespoon kirsch

- Brandied Peppermint Fondue

- Pineapple slices and cake pieces for dipping

Directions

1. Combine both fondues and place in a bowl over a saucepan filled with barely simmering water. Add the coconut milk and the kirsch.

2. Transfer the fondue mixture to the fondue pot and set on the burner. Keep the fondue warm on low heat. Serve with the pineapple slices and cake for dipping.

Sweet, Sour, and Spicy Apple

Ingredients

- 2 Spartan apples

- 1 tablespoon brown sugar

- ¼ teaspoon cinnamon

- ½ cup apple juice

- 4 tablespoons honey

- 2 teaspoons apple schnapps, optional

- 2 tablespoons balsamic vinegar

- 3 tablespoons butter or margarine, divided

Directions

1. Wash, core, and cut the apples into thin slices. Toss the sliced apples with the cinnamon. Warm the honey and balsamic vinegar in a medium saucepan.

2. While the honey and vinegar are warming, heat 2 tablespoons of the butter or margarine in a pan. Sauté the apple slices until they are tender. Add the remaining tablespoon of butter and the brown sugar. Cook until the brown sugar has caramelized.

3. Add the apple juice to the honey-and-vinegar mixture. When it has warmed, add the apple slices and heat the mixture. If using the liqueur, stir it in and allow to cook for another few minutes. Transfer to a fondue pot and set up the burner. Use a dipping fork to pick up the apple slices.

Red, White, and Blue Fondue

Ingredients

- 4 cups mixed frozen raspberries and blueberries

- 4 teaspoons cornstarch

- 4 teaspoons water

- 6 tablespoons sugar

- 2 tablespoons kirsch

- 1 tablespoon lemon juice

- 20–24 ladyfingers

- 1 cup plain yogurt

Directions

1. Heat the berries on medium-low heat with the sugar, stirring, until they are mushy. Stir in the lemon juice. Process in a blender or food processor.

2. Return the berries to the saucepan on medium-low heat and add the yogurt. Dissolve the cornstarch in the water and add to the yogurt mixture, stirring to thicken. Stir in the kirsch.

3. Transfer the fondue mixture to the fondue pot and set on the burner. Keep the fondue warm on low heat. Serve with the ladyfingers for dipping.

Doughnut Fondue

Ingredients

- 8 ounces semisweet chocolate

- ¼ cup half-and-half

- 1 cup cinnamon baking chips

- 2 tablespoons butter or margarine

- 6 tablespoons sour cream

- ¼ teaspoon ground allspice

- 6 tablespoons evaporated milk

- Plain doughnuts for dipping

Directions

1. Break the chocolate into pieces. Combine the chocolate, baking chips, sour cream,

evaporated milk, and half-and-half in a metal bowl and place on top of a saucepan half-filled with simmering water. Melt the mixture on low to medium-low heat, making sure that it doesn't boil. Add the butter or margarine and melt. Stir in the ground allspice.

2. Transfer the fondue mixture to the fondue pot and set on the burner. Keep the fondue warm on low heat. Serve with the doughnuts for dipping. The doughnuts can be eaten whole or cut into pieces and speared with a dipping fork.

Fondue with Tangerines

Ingredients

- 6 tangerines
- 1½ tablespoons kirsch
- 2 cups semisweet chocolate chips
- ½ cup half-and-half or light cream

Directions

1. Peel the tangerines and dry on paper towels. Combine the chocolate chips and cream in a metal bowl and place on top of a saucepan half-filled with simmering water. Melt the mixture on low to medium-low heat, making sure that it doesn't boil. Stir in the kirsch.

2. Transfer the fondue mixture to the fondue pot and set on the burner. Keep the fondue warm on low heat. Serve with the tangerine slices for dipping.

Sweet Pudding

Ingredients

- 6 bananas
- 4 tablespoons sugar
- 1½ cups cocoa
- 4 tablespoons butter or margarine
- 6 tablespoons corn syrup
- ½ cup milk

Directions

1. Peel the bananas and cut into 1-inch pieces. Combine the cocoa, corn syrup, milk, and sugar.

2. Melt the butter in a medium saucepan. Add the cocoa-and-milk mixture. Bring to a boil and simmer for 10 minutes. Remove and cool. The pudding will thicken as it cools. Serve with the bananas for dipping.

Homemade Butterscotch Fondue

Ingredients

- 2 cups sugar

- 2 tablespoons corn syrup

- ½ cup water

- ½ cup unsalted peanuts, chopped

- 4 tablespoons butter

- Marshmallows, fruit, or cake for dipping

- ½ cup whipping cream

Directions

1. Combine the sugar and water in a medium saucepan and cook on medium heat, stirring to dissolve the sugar. When the sugar is dissolved, turn up the heat and boil the mixture for at least 5 minutes, until the sugar turns a golden color.

2. If the sugar has formed clumps, leave on medium heat and stir to melt the clumps. Once the butterscotch is evenly mixed, remove from the heat and immediately stir in the butter and the whipping cream. Stir vigorously to keep the mixture from hardening. Stir in the corn syrup and the chopped peanuts. Serve unheated in a bowl with the marshmallows, fruit, or cake for dipping.

Tiramisu with Cream

Ingredients

- 1 pound mascarpone

- 2 teaspoons cornstarch

- ¼ cup light cream

- 2 tablespoons rum

- ¼ cup powdered (confectioners' or icing) sugar

- 4 egg yolks

- 2 teaspoons cinnamon

- ¼ cup strong, fresh brewed espresso coffee

- 24 ladyfingers

- 1 tablespoon plus 1 teaspoon powdered hot chocolate

Directions

1. Combine the mascarpone, light cream, powdered sugar, and 4 teaspoons of the espresso in a metal bowl and place on top of a saucepan half-filled with simmering water. Melt the mixture on low to medium-low heat, stirring frequently and making sure that it doesn't boil.

2. When the mascarpone has melted and has a texture close to pudding, stir in the hot chocolate. Dissolve the cornstarch in the rum and stir into the fondue. Whisk in the egg yolks to thicken.

3. Transfer the fondue mixture to the fondue pot and set on the burner. Keep warm on low heat. Just before serving, sprinkle with the cinnamon. Brush the ladyfingers with the remainder of the espresso and serve with the fondue for dipping.

Fruit Fiesta

Ingredients

- 1 pound plums

- 1 teaspoon lemon juice

- 1 medium mango

- ½ teaspoon ground ginger

- 1 cup water

- ½ teaspoon cinnamon

- ½ cup sugar

Directions

1. Wash and drain the fruit. Cut the plums in half, remove the stem and pit, and cut in half again. Cut off the stem of the mango and peel. Cut in half, remove the pit, and cut the flesh into bite-sized chunks.

2. In a medium saucepan, warm the water on medium-low heat. (Note: If using canned mangoes

or plums, feel free to replace a few tablespoons of the water with the canned fruit juice.) Turn up the heat until nearly boiling and add the sugar, stirring to dissolve. Add the mango and simmer for a few minutes.

3. Add the plums and simmer for 20 minutes more. Stir in the lemon juice, ginger, and cinnamon. Simmer for a few more minutes, then process in a blender or food processor. Transfer the fruit mixture to a fondue pot and set on the burner over medium heat to keep the fruit warm.

Deep-Fried Ice Cream

Ingredients

- ½ cup graham cracker crumbs

- Quick and Easy Batter

- ½ teaspoon nutmeg

- 4 tablespoons plus 2 teaspoons sugar

- 1 teaspoon cinnamon

- 4 cups oil, or as needed

- 1 pint vanilla ice cream

Directions

1. Line a tray with aluminum foil. Place in the freezer while preparing the crumb coating. Combine the graham cracker crumbs, nutmeg, and 1 tablespoon plus 2 teaspoons of the sugar and set aside.

2. Scoop out 6 golf-ball-sized scoops of ice cream. Roll thoroughly in the crumb mixture. Stick a chopstick through the middle of each ball, and place on the frozen tray. Freeze overnight.

3. The next day, prepare the batter. Refrigerate and chill for 30 minutes. Combine the cinnamon with 3 tablespoons of the sugar and set aside. Heat the oil in the fondue pot on the stove, and set on the burner.

4. Take one ice cream ball out of the freezer. If necessary, use a knife to gently dislodge the bottom of the ball from the foil. Use your fingers to completely coat the ball with the batter.

5. If possible, lay the chopstick across the fondue pot, so that half the ice cream is in the hot oil.

(This works best with an electric fondue pot.) Otherwise, use a dipping basket to gently lower the ice cream ball until it is submerged halfway in the oil. Cook very briefly, for about 5 seconds, then turn over and cook the other side. Remove and roll in the cinnamon mixture. Continue with the rest of the ice cream balls.

Decadent Mascarpone Fondue

Ingredients

- 1 pound mascarpone
- 4 teaspoons powdered hot chocolate
- ¼ cup light cream
- ¼ cup powdered (confectioners' or icing) sugar
- 2 teaspoons cornstarch
- 2 tablespoons brandy

Directions

1. Combine the mascarpone, cream, and powdered sugar in a metal bowl and place on top of a saucepan half-filled with simmering water. Melt the mixture on low to medium-low heat, stirring frequently and making sure that it doesn't boil.

2. When the cheese has melted and has a texture close to pudding, stir in the hot chocolate. Dissolve the cornstarch in the brandy and stir into the fondue.

3. Transfer the fondue mixture to the fondue pot and set on the burner. Keep warm on low heat.

Sour Cream Fondue

Ingredients

- 2 cups canned pineapple chunks
- 3 tablespoons liquid honey
- 3 tablespoons pineapple juice (reserved from the can)
- 1½ cups sour cream

Directions

1. Dry the pineapple chunks. Combine the sour cream, honey, and pineapple juice. Chill briefly until the fondue just starts to set. Use dipping forks to dip the pineapple chunks into the sour cream.

Chocolate Zucchini Fondue

Ingredients

- 4 zucchini

- 1 teaspoon almond extract

- 1¾ cups chocolate chips

- 1 tablespoon plus 1 teaspoon instant hot chocolate

- ⅓ cup plus 2 tablespoons evaporated milk

- ½ teaspoon cinnamon

- 2 teaspoons vanilla extract

- 1 tablespoon kirsch

Directions

1. Wash the zucchini, peel, and cut diagonally into slices approximately ¼–½ inch thick. Cut in half again.

2. Combine the chocolate chips, evaporated milk, vanilla extract, and almond extract in a metal bowl and place on top of a saucepan half-filled with simmering water. Melt the chocolate on low to medium-low heat, stirring frequently and making sure that it doesn't boil. Stir in the cocoa, cinnamon, and kirsch.

3. Transfer the fondue mixture to the fondue pot and set on the burner. Keep the fondue warm on low heat. Serve with the zucchini slices for dipping.

Sweet Orange Liqueur Fondue

Ingredients

- 1 pound nectarines

- 1 teaspoon vanilla extract

- 1 pound fresh peaches

- 20 mini marshmallows

- 8 ounces semisweet chocolate

- 1 tablespoon Grand Marnier

- 1 cup whipping cream

- 4 French madeleine cookies, optional

- ½ teaspoon almond extract

Directions

1. Wash the nectarines and peaches and dry thoroughly. Remove the pits and cut each piece of fruit into 6 to 8 equal wedges.

2. Break the chocolate into pieces. Combine the chocolate, whipping cream, almond extract, vanilla extract, and marshmallows in a metal bowl and place on top of a saucepan half-filled with simmering water. Melt the chocolate on low heat. Stir in the Grand Marnier.

3. Transfer the fondue mixture to the fondue pot and set on the burner. Keep the fondue warm on low heat. Use dipping forks to spear the fruit wedges and draw through the chocolate. Serve with the cookies.

Basic Chocolate Chip Fondue for Two

Ingredients

- 1¼ cups chocolate chips

- 2 teaspoons liqueur

- ⅓ cup light cream

- 3 cups fresh fruit for dipping

Directions

1. Combine the chocolate chips and cream in a metal bowl and place on top of a saucepan half-filled with simmering water. Melt the chocolate on low to medium-low heat, stirring frequently and making sure that it doesn't boil. Stir in the liqueur.

2. Transfer the fondue mixture to the fondue pot and set on the burner. Keep the fondue warm on low heat. Serve with fresh fruit slices for dipping. Use dipping forks to spear the pieces of fruit and draw them through the warm chocolate.

Summer Squash Fondue

Ingredients

- 2 zucchini

- 1 tablespoon instant hot chocolate

- 1¼ cups chocolate chips

- ⅓ cup evaporated milk

- 2 teaspoons kirsch, or to taste

- 1 teaspoon vanilla extract

Directions

1. Wash and peel the zucchini. Cut diagonally into slices approximately ¼–½ inch thick.

2. Combine the chocolate chips, evaporated milk, and vanilla extract in a metal bowl and place on top of a saucepan half-filled with simmering water. Melt the chocolate on low to medium-low heat, stirring frequently and making sure that it doesn't boil. Stir in the cocoa and kirsch.

3. Transfer the fondue mixture to the fondue pot and set on the burner. Keep the fondue warm on low heat. Serve with the sliced zucchini for dipping.

Macaroons Dipped in White Chocolate

Ingredients

- 30–40 coconut macaroons

- 2 tablespoons whipping cream

- 2 cups frozen red and blue berries

- 4 teaspoons cornstarch

- 4½ teaspoons water

- 3 tablespoons sugar

- 2 teaspoons coconut flakes

- 1 teaspoon lemon juice

- 2 tablespoons cognac

- 4 ounces white chocolate

Directions

1. One hour before preparing the fondue, place the macaroons in the refrigerator.

2. Break up any large frozen berries, such as strawberries, into pieces. Heat the berries on medium-low heat with the sugar, stirring, until they are mushy. Stir in the lemon juice. Process in a blender or food processor.

3. Break the white chocolate into pieces. Combine the whipping cream and 2 ounces of chocolate in a metal bowl and place on top of a saucepan half-filled with simmering water. Melt the chocolate on low to medium-low heat, stirring frequently and making sure that it doesn't boil.

4. Add the strained berries and add the remaining 2 ounces of white chocolate. Dissolve the cornstarch in the water. When all the chocolate has melted, add the cornstarch-and-water mixture, stirring to thicken. Stir in the coconut and the cognac.

5. Transfer the fondue mixture to the fondue pot and set on the burner. Keep the fondue warm on low heat. Serve with the macaroons for dipping.

Almond Orange Fondue

Ingredients

- 3 tangerines
- ¼ teaspoon grated orange peel
- 6 ounces semisweet chocolate
- 2 teaspoons orange liqueur
- ¾ cup whipping cream
- 4 almond cookies
- ¼ teaspoon almond extract

Directions

1. Peel the tangerines, separate into segments, and pat dry on paper towels. Break the chocolate into pieces.

2. Combine the whipping cream, chocolate, almond extract, and grated orange peel in a metal bowl and place on top of a saucepan half-filled with simmering water. Melt the chocolate on low to medium-low heat, stirring frequently and making sure that it doesn't boil. Stir in the orange liqueur.

3. Transfer the fondue mixture to the fondue pot and set on the burner. Keep the fondue warm on low heat. Serve with the tangerines and almond cookies for dipping.

Brandied Peppermint Fondue

Ingredients

- 8 caramel candies
- ¾ cup peppermint chips
- ⅓ cup half-and-half
- 1½ tablespoons kirsch
- 1 cup semisweet chocolate chips
- 15–20 cookies

Directions

1. Unwrap the caramel candies. Combine the half-and-half and caramels in a metal bowl and place on top of a saucepan half-filled with simmering water. When the caramels are half-melted, add the chocolate and peppermint chips.

2. Melt the mixture on low heat, stirring continuously, and making sure that it doesn't boil. When the chocolate is melted, stir in the kirsch.

3. Transfer the fondue mixture to the fondue pot and set on the burner. Keep the fondue warm on low heat. Serve with the cookies for dipping

Honey Almond Flambé

Ingredients

- 4 3.5-ounce Toblerone Honey and Almond milk chocolate bars
- 2 tablespoons cognac
- Banana and pear slices for dipping, as needed
- ½ cup half-and-half or light cream

Directions

1. Break the chocolate into pieces. Combine the chocolate and cream in a metal bowl placed over a saucepan half-filled with boiling water. When the chocolate is melted, transfer the fondue mixture to the fondue pot and set on the burner.

2. Add the cognac on top of the fondue, reserving 1 teaspoon. Fill a dessert spoon with the 1 teaspoon of cognac. Light the cognac on the spoon. Use the lighted cognac to light the brandy on the chocolate. Once the cognac has burned out, the fondue is ready to eat.

3. Keep the fondue warm on low heat. Serve with the fresh fruit slices for dipping.

Instant Fondue

Ingredients

- ¼ cup walnuts, finely chopped

- ½ pound Cheddar cheese

- 2 tablespoons apple schnapps

- Crackers for dipping

Directions

1. Preheat the oven to 350°F. Soak the walnuts in the liqueur for at least 15 minutes.

2. Slice the Cheddar and break into chunks. Lay out flat in a shallow greased baking dish. Sprinkle the liquor-soaked walnuts on top.

3. Bake for 3 to 5 minutes, until the cheese melts. (This will happen quite quickly.) Remove and serve in a ceramic fondue pot, with the crackers for dipping.

Deep-Fried Chocolate

Ingredients

- 1 3.5-ounce Toblerone bar

- ¼ cup Tempura Batter (), prepared without the black pepper

- 1 egg, lightly beaten

- ⅓ cup graham cracker crumbs

- 4½ cups oil, or as needed

Directions

1. Break the Toblerone bar into 12 individual pieces. Dip each piece in the beaten egg and then roll in the graham cracker crumbs until coated. Place the chocolate on a tray lined with aluminum foil and freeze for 2 hours.

2. Add the oil to the fondue pot, making sure it is not more than half full. Heat the pot on a

stove element over medium-high heat.

3. When the oil is hot, move the fondue pot to the table and set up the burner. Coat the chocolate with the batter, using your fingers. Using a dipping basket or spatula, gently lower the chocolate into the hot oil. Cook very briefly until the batter lightly browns (about 30 seconds). Eat immediately.

Blushing Fondue

Ingredients

- ½ pound Swiss Emmenthal cheese

- 2 teaspoons lemon juice

- 1½ tablespoons cornstarch

- ½ pound Gruyère cheese

- 2 tablespoons kirsch

- 1 garlic clove

- ½ teaspoon nutmeg

- 1 cup dry rosé

- ½ loaf French bread, cubed

Directions

1. Finely dice the Emmenthal and Gruyère cheeses and set aside. Smash the garlic, peel, and cut in half.

2. Rub the garlic around the inside of a medium saucepan. Discard. Add the rosé to the pan and cook on low heat. Don't allow the wine to boil.

3. When the rosé is warm, stir in the lemon juice. Add the cheese, a handful at a time. Stir the cheese continually in a sideways figure eight pattern. Wait until the cheese is completely melted before adding more. Don't allow the fondue mixture to boil.

4. When the cheese is melted, turn up the heat until it is just bubbling and starting to thicken. Dissolve the cornstarch in the kirsch and add to the cheese. Stir in the nutmeg. Transfer to a fondue pot and set on the burner. Serve with the French bread cubes for dipping.

Champagne Fondue

Ingredients

- 1 pound Brie cheese
- 2 teaspoons cornstarch
- 1 garlic clove
- 1/8 teaspoon nutmeg, or to taste
- 1 cup plus 2 tablespoons dry champagne
- 1 French bread baguette, cut into cubes
- 2 teaspoons lemon juice

Directions

1. Cut the Brie into cubes. Smash the garlic, peel, and cut in half. Rub the garlic around the inside of a medium saucepan. Discard. Add 1 cup champagne to the saucepan and warm on medium-low heat. Don't allow it to boil.

2. When the champagne is warm, stir in the lemon juice. Add the cheese, a few cubes at a time. Stir the cheese continually in a sideways figure eight pattern. Wait until the cheese is completely melted before adding more. Don't allow the fondue mixture to boil.

3. Dissolve the cornstarch in the remaining 2 tablespoons of champagne. When the cheese is melted, add the dissolved cornstarch. Turn up the heat until it is just bubbling and starting to thicken. Stir in the nutmeg.

4. Transfer to a fondue pot and set on the burner. Serve with the sliced French baguette cubes for dipping.

Tiramisu for Two

Ingredients

- ½ pound mascarpone
- 1 teaspoon cornstarch
- 1 teaspoon cornstarch
- 1 tablespoon rum
- 2 tablespoons powdered (confectioners' or icing) sugar
- 2 egg yolks

- 1 teaspoon cinnamon

- 2 tablespoons strong hot coffee, divided

- 12 ladyfingers

- 2 teaspoons powdered hot chocolate

Directions

1. Combine the mascarpone, cream, powdered sugar, and 2 teaspoons of the coffee in a metal bowl and place on top of a saucepan half-filled with simmering water. Melt the mixture on low to medium-low heat, stirring frequently and making sure that it doesn't boil.

2. When the mascarpone has melted and has a texture close to pudding, stir in the hot chocolate. Dissolve the cornstarch in the rum and stir into the fondue. Whisk in the egg yolks to thicken.

3. Transfer the fondue mixture to the fondue pot and set on the burner. Keep warm on low heat. Just before serving, sprinkle with the cinnamon. Brush the ladyfingers with the remainder of the coffee and serve with the fondue for dipping.

French Crème Fraîche Fondue

Ingredients

- ½ cup heavy cream

- 8 ounces semisweet chocolate

- 1 tablespoon buttermilk

- 2 tablespoons coffee liqueur

- 2 apples

Biscotti

- 2 teaspoons lemon juice

Directions

1. The day before you plan to serve the fondue, make the crème fraîche. Combine the heavy cream and buttermilk in a bowl, cover, and let sit for 24 hours.

2. Wash the apples and dry thoroughly. Cut the apples in half, remove the stems and seeds, and cut each apple into 6 to 8 equal wedges. Lightly brush the wedges with lemon juice and refrigerate.

3. Combine the semisweet chocolate and the crème fraîche in a metal bowl placed on top of a saucepan half-filled with simmering water. Melt the chocolate on low heat, stirring frequently and making sure that it doesn't boil. Stir in the coffee liqueur.

4. Transfer the fondue mixture to the fondue pot and set on the burner. Keep warm on low heat. Serve with the biscotti and apple wedges for dipping.

Chocolate-Honey Fondue

Ingredients

- 4 bananas

- 2 teaspoons liquid honey

- 4 ounces unsweetened chocolate

- 1 tablespoon honey liqueur

- ⅔ cup sweetened condensed milk

Directions

1. Peel the bananas and slice. Refrigerate until it is time to use the bananas in the fondue.

2. Combine the unsweetened chocolate, condensed milk, and honey in a metal bowl placed on top of a saucepan half-filled with simmering water. Melt the chocolate on low heat, stirring frequently and making sure that it doesn't boil. Remove from the heat and stir in the honey liqueur.

3. Transfer the fondue mixture to the fondue pot and set on the burner. Keep warm on low heat. Serve with the banana slices for dipping.

Mascarpone with Baked Pears

Ingredients

- 4–6 firm ripe pears

- ⅛ teaspoon nutmeg

- ¾ cup apple juice

- ¼ teaspoon cinnamon, or to taste

- 8 ounces mascarpone

- ¼ cup corn syrup

- 3 teaspoons rum

Directions

1. Preheat oven to 350°F. Cut the pears in half, remove the stems and seeds, and cut into bite-sized chunks. Place in a 9″ × 9″ shallow glass dish and pour the apple juice over. Bake for 30 minutes.

2. Combine the mascarpone and corn syrup in a metal bowl and place on top of a saucepan half-filled with simmering water. Melt the mixture on low to medium-low heat, stirring frequently and making sure that it doesn't boil. When the mascarpone has melted and the fondue has the texture of custard, stir in the nutmeg, cinnamon, and rum.

3. Transfer the fondue mixture to a dessert fondue pot and keep warm on low heat over a candle. Use dipping forks to spear the baked pear chunks and dip into the fondue.

Peppermint Fondue

Ingredients

- 4 ounces semisweet chocolate

- 1 tablespoon butter or margarine

- ½ cup peppermint-flavored baking chips

- 1 tablespoon peppermint liqueur, or to taste

- 3 tablespoons sour cream

- 6 teaspoons evaporated milk

Directions

1. Combine the semisweet chocolate, peppermint baking chips, sour cream, and evaporated milk in a metal bowl and place on top of a saucepan half-filled with simmering water. Melt the chocolate on low to medium-low heat, stirring frequently and making sure that it doesn't boil. Add the butter or margarine and melt. Stir in the peppermint liqueur.

2. Transfer the fondue mixture to the fondue pot and set on the burner. Keep the fondue warm on low heat. Serve with fresh fruit slices for dipping.

Dim Sum for Two

Ingredients

- 4 frozen gyoza pork potstickers
- 4½ cups oil, or as needed Golden Hot Mustard
- 4 frozen prawn potstickers
- 2 frozen spring rolls
- ¼ cup soy sauce

Directions

1. Thaw the potstickers and spring rolls. Pat dry with paper towels to remove any excess moisture.

2. Add the oil to the fondue pot, making sure it is not more than half full. Heat the pot on a stove element over medium-high heat. When the oil is hot, move the fondue pot to the table and set up the burner.

3. Use dipping forks to spear the potstickers and spring rolls. Cook in the hot oil until they turn golden brown. Serve with the mustard and soy sauce for dipping.

Fried Ice Cream with Decadent Chocolate Sauce

Ingredients

- Vanilla ice cream
- ½ cup semisweet chocolate chips
- ⅓ cup graham cracker crumbs
- ¾ cup Quick and Easy Batter
- ¼ cup evaporated milk
- 1 tablespoon liquid honey
- 4½ cups oil, or as needed
- ½ teaspoon vanilla extract

Directions

1. Cover a tray with aluminum foil, and place in the freezer. Form 4 large scoops of ice cream the size of tennis balls. Roll each ball in the graham cracker crumbs, making sure it is thoroughly covered. (You may have graham cracker crumbs left over.) Stick a chopstick

through the middle of each ball. Place on the tray and freeze overnight.

2. Chill the batter in the refrigerator for 30 minutes. Heat the oil in the fondue pot on the stove, and set on the burner.

3. While the oil is heating, prepare the sauce. Combine the chocolate chips, evaporated milk, honey, and vanilla extract in a metal bowl placed over a saucepan half-filled with boiling water. Melt the chocolate and allow to cool.

4. Take 1 ice cream ball out of the freezer. If necessary, use a knife to gently dislodge the bottom of the ball from the foil. Use your fingers to completely coat the ball with the batter. Maneuver the chopstick so that only the bottom half of the ice cream is in the hot oil. (Use a spatula or dipping basket if necessary.) Cook very briefly, for about 5 seconds, then turn over and cook the other side. Remove and dip into the chocolate sauce. Continue with the rest of the ice cream balls.

Fried Cheese Cubes

Ingredients

- ¾ pound Fontina cheese

- ¼ teaspoon paprika

- 1 cup bran flakes

- ½ teaspoon sugar

- 2 eggs

- 4½ cups oil, or as needed

- 1 tablespoon milk

- ½ cup flour

Directions

1. Remove the rind from the cheese and cut into cubes about ¾ inch thick.

2. Crush the bran flakes with a mortar and pestle. Beat the eggs with the milk, paprika, and sugar. Make sure the eggs are thoroughly beaten. Use your hands to mix the crushed bran flakes with the beaten eggs.

3. Add the oil to the fondue pot, making sure it is not more than half full. Heat the pot on a

stove element over medium-high heat.

4. When the oil is hot, move the fondue pot to the table and set up the burner. Coat the cheese cubes with the flour. Dip the cheese into the egg mixture, making sure it is thoroughly coated. Spear the cheese with a dipping fork and cook very briefly in the hot oil. Drain on paper towels if desired. Cool and eat.

Spring Rolls for Two

Ingredients

- ½ cup baby shrimp
- 1 large Chinese dried mushroom, sliced, optional
- 1 tablespoon plus 2 teaspoons oyster sauce
- 1 green onion
- ½ tablespoon water
- 5 cups oil, or as needed
- 1 tablespoon soy sauce
- ¼ teaspoon sesame oil
- ½ teaspoon sugar
- 4–6 spring roll wrappers
- ½ cup mung bean sprouts
- 2 tablespoons cornstarch mixed with 1 tablespoon water
- ½ carrot
- 1 tablespoon canned bamboo shoots

Directions

1. Rinse the shrimp and pat dry. Cut into tiny pieces. Toss with 2 teaspoons of the oyster sauce and let marinate for 15 minutes. Mix together the water, 1 tablespoon oyster sauce, soy sauce, and sugar. Set aside.

2. Rinse the mung bean sprouts and drain thoroughly. Wash and grate the carrot until you have 2 full tablespoons. Cut the bamboo shoots in half and then cut into very thin slices. Dice the green onion.

3. Add 1½ tablespoons vegetable oil to a frying pan. When oil is hot, add the dried mushroom slices. Fry for about 1 minute, then add the bamboo shoots, bean sprouts, grated carrot, and the green onion. Mix in the soy sauce mixture and bring to a boil. Add the shrimp. Drizzle with the sesame oil. Cool.

4. To prepare the spring rolls, lay a wrapper in front of you so that it forms 2 triangles. Use your fingers to brush the edges of the wrapper with the cornstarch-and-water mixture. Place a full tablespoon of filling in the middle. Roll up the wrapper, tucking in the edges, and seal with more cornstarch and water. Prepare the remaining spring rolls in the same way.

5. Add the oil to the fondue pot, making sure it is not more than half full. Heat the pot on a stove element over medium-high heat. When the oil is hot, move the fondue pot to the table and set up the burner. Deep-fry the spring rolls, two at a time, until they turn golden. Drain on paper towels.

Carpaccio-Style Beef with Pesto Mayonnaise

Ingredients

- 4 ounces beef tenderloin, sliced paper thin
- 2 tablespoons freshly cracked black pepper
- 2 ounces Parmigiano-Reggiano cheese
- ¼ cup fresh basil leaves, chopped
- 1 tablespoon olive or vegetable oil
- Pesto Mayonnaise
- ½ Italian or French baguette, sliced
- 2 tablespoons lemon juice
- 2 tablespoons extra-virgin olive oil

Directions

1. Keep the beef chilled until ready to use. Shred the Parmigiano-Reggiano cheese.

2. Place the beef between pieces of lightly oiled plastic wrap. Pound with a mallet to thin the beef even further. Remove the beef from the wrap and brush on both sides with the lemon

juice. Refrigerate for 1 hour.

3. Cut the beef into thin strips. Lightly brush with the extra-virgin olive oil and sprinkle the cracked black pepper over. Place on a serving dish and garnish with the fresh basil leaves and shredded cheese.

4. Place the mayonnaise in a cheese or dessert fondue bowl in the middle of the table. Skewer the beef slices and dip into the mayonnaise. Eat with the baguette slices.

Tandoori-Style Chicken Wings

Ingredients

- 2 pounds chicken wings Instant Tandoori Rub

- 2 teaspoons lemon juice

- 5 cups oil, or as needed

- 1 cup sour cream

- 1 lemon, optional

- 1 cup plain yogurt

Directions

1. Rinse the chicken wings and pat dry. Cut through the wings at the joint. Rub the Tandoori Rub into the chicken.

2. Combine the sour cream with the yogurt. Stir in the lemon juice. Place in individual serving dishes and refrigerate until ready to serve.

3. Add the oil to the fondue pot, making sure it is not more than half full. Heat the pot on a stove element over medium-high heat.

4. When the oil is hot, move the fondue pot to the table and set up the burner. Use dipping forks or metal skewers to skewer the chicken wings. Cook in the hot oil until the wings are browned and cooked through. Drain on paper towels or use a tempura rack if desired. Serve with the yogurt and sour cream mixture for dipping.

Chicken Egg Rolls

Ingredients

- 4 ounces chicken meat

- 4 dried Chinese mushrooms
- 1 teaspoon Chinese cooking wine
- 1 tablespoon bamboo shoots, shredded
- ¼ teaspoon sesame oil
- 2 teaspoons water
- 2 tablespoons plus 1 teaspoon red bell pepper, finely diced
- 1 tablespoon plus 1 teaspoon oyster sauce
- 4 cups oil, or as needed
- 1 teaspoon soy sauce
- 10 egg roll wrappers
- ½ teaspoon sugar
- 4 tablespoons cornstarch mixed with 2 tablespoons water
- ½ carrot

Directions

1. Chop the chicken meat. Add the Chinese cooking wine and a few drops of sesame oil and marinate the chicken for 30 minutes. Mix together the water, oyster sauce, soy sauce, and sugar. Set aside.

2. Wash or rinse all the vegetables and drain thoroughly. Grate the carrot until you have 2 tablespoons plus 1 teaspoon. Soak the Chinese dried mushrooms in warm water for at least 20 minutes to soften. Squeeze out the excess water, remove the stems, and thinly slice. Mix together the grated carrot, mushrooms, bamboo shoots, and bell pepper.

3. Add 2 tablespoons vegetable oil to a frying pan. When oil is hot, add the chicken. Fry until it changes color, then add the vegetables. Mix in the sauce and bring to a boil. Drizzle with the remaining sesame oil. Cool.

4. To prepare the egg rolls, lay a wrapper in front of you so that it forms a square. Use your fingers to brush all the edges of the wrapper with the cornstarch-and-water mixture. Place a heaping tablespoon of filling in the middle. Fold the top of the wrapper over the filling, fold the bottom half over the top, and seal the edges with more cornstarch and water. Seal the side

edges, fold over, and seal again. Continue preparing the remainder of the egg rolls.

5. Add the remainder of the oil to the fondue pot, making sure it is not more than half full. Heat the pot on the stove over medium-high heat. When the oil is hot, move the fondue pot to the table and set up the burner. Deep-fry the egg rolls, two at a time, until they turn golden. Drain.

Chicken and Vegetables Bathed in Broth

Ingredients

- 2 skinless, boneless chicken breasts (about 10 ounces each)
- 2 portobello mushrooms
- 6 cups Homemade Chicken Broth
- 1 green bell pepper
- 2 slices ginger
- 1 red bell pepper
- Sour Cream and Mustard Dip
- 2 zucchini
- 2 stalks celery
- ½ cup hot chili sauce
- 1 tomato

Directions

1. Rinse the chicken and pat dry. Cut into thin strips.

2. Wash all the vegetables and drain thoroughly. Cut the bell peppers in half, remove the stem and seeds, and cut into bite-sized cubes. Cut the zucchini and the celery into 1-inch pieces. Cut the tomato into 6 to 8 wedges. Thinly slice the portobello mushrooms.

3. Heat the broth on the stove with the ginger slices and bring to a boil. Transfer enough broth to fill the fondue pot about ⅔ full. Set the fondue pot on the burner, with enough heat to keep the broth simmering throughout the meal. (Keep the remaining broth warm on the stove to use as needed.)4. Use dipping forks to spear the chicken and vegetables and cook in the hot broth. Serve with the mustard dip and the hot chili sauce for dipping.

Chicken with Curried Rice

Ingredients

- 3 cups cooked chicken meat

- ¾ teaspoon curry powder

- ½ pound fresh spinach leaves

- ¾ teaspoon ground cumin

- 2 tablespoons olive oil

- ⅔ cup raisins

- ¼ onion, peeled and chopped

- Curried Yogurt

- 2 cups long-grain rice

- 1 cup plain yogurt

- 8 cups Homemade Chicken Broth (

Directions

1. Cut the chicken into bite-sized pieces that can be easily speared with a dipping fork. Set aside. Wash the spinach and drain thoroughly.

2. Heat the olive oil in a frying pan over low heat. Add the chopped onion and cook until soft. Add the rice and sauté for 5 minutes until it turns shiny and is heated through.

3. Add 3 cups of broth to the rice. Add the curry powder, ground cumin, and raisins. Bring the rice to a boil, uncovered, on medium heat. Cover, turn down the heat, and boil until cooked through, stirring occasionally. Keep the rice warm over low heat.

4. Bring the remaining 5 cups of broth to a boil on the stove. Add the spinach and simmer briefly. Set the fondue pot on the burner, with enough heat to keep the broth simmering throughout the meal. Cook the chicken and spinach leaves briefly in the broth (use a fondue dipping basket for the spinach leaves if desired). Serve with the Curried Yogurt and plain yogurt for dipping. Eat with the curried rice.

Chicken Bourguignonne

Ingredients

- 4 skinless, boneless chicken breasts (about 6 ounces each)

- 2 green bell peppers

- Mediterranean Chicken Marinade

- 2 red bell peppers

- 8 ounces fresh small mushrooms

- Lemon-Soy Dressing Freshly ground black pepper, as needed

Directions

1. Rinse the chicken breasts and pat dry. Cut into cubes about 1 inch thick. Place the cubed chicken in a shallow glass dish and brush the marinade over with a pastry brush. Refrigerate and marinate the chicken for 1 hour.

2. Wipe the mushrooms clean with a damp cloth. Dry and cut each mushroom in half.

3. Wash the bell peppers and dry thoroughly. Cut in half, remove the seeds, and cut into cubes between ¾ and 1 inch thick.

4. Add the oil to the fondue pot, making sure it is not more than half full. Heat the pot on a stove element over medium-high heat. When the oil is hot, move the fondue pot to the table, set on the burner, and maintain the heat.

5. Set the chicken and vegetables on serving dishes at the table. Use metal skewers with wooden handles and invite guests to spear 1 pepper, mushrooms, and a chicken cube and cook in the hot oil until the chicken changes color and is cooked through. Drain on paper towels or a tempura rack if desired. Serve with the Lemon-Soy Dressing and freshly ground black pepper for dipping.

Spicy Fried Chicken with Mushrooms

Ingredients

- 12 skinless, boneless chicken thighs

- 7 cups oil, or as needed Speedy Garlic Mayonnaise

- Simple Chicken Rub

- 4 potatoes

- Lemon-Soy Dressing

- 2 green bell peppers
- Horseradish Cream
- 2 red bell peppers
- ¾ pound fresh small mushrooms

Directions

1. Rinse the chicken thighs, pat dry, and cover with the chicken rub. Cut into cubes.

2. Boil the potatoes for about 15 minutes over medium-low heat, until they can be pierced with a fork but are not too soft. Drain thoroughly, and cut lengthwise into pieces approximately ¾ inch thick.

3. Wash the bell peppers and dry thoroughly. Cut in half, remove the seeds, and cut into strips approximately ¾ inch thick. Wipe the mushrooms with a damp cloth and cut off the stems.

4. Add the oil to the fondue pot, making sure it is not more than half full. Heat the pot on a stove element over medium-high heat. When the oil is hot, move the fondue pot to the table, set on the burner, and maintain the heat.

5. Set the chicken cubes, mushrooms, potatoes, and bell peppers on the table. Use dipping forks or metal skewers with wooden handles to spear 1 or more pieces of food and cook in the hot oil until cooked. Be sure to cook the chicken until it changes color. Drain on paper towels or a tempura rack if desired. Serve with the Speedy Garlic Mayonnaise for the chicken, Lemon-Soy Dressing for the mushrooms, and Horseradish Cream for the potatoes. (Eat the peppers as is or with the dip of your choice.)

Chicken Hot Pot Style

Ingredients

- 4 skinless, boneless chicken breasts
- 1 garlic clove
- 1 8-ounce can bamboo shoots
- 8 ounces cellophane noodles
- 1 8-ounce can water chestnuts
- 6 ounces bok choy

- Basic Mongolian Hot Pot Broth

- 2 green onions

- 3 slices ginger

Directions

1. Cut the chicken into 1-inch cubes. Place on a serving tray on the table, along with dipping sauces. Make sure to give each guest an individual soup bowl when setting the table.

2. Rinse the cellophane noodles and cover with warm water for 15 minutes to soften. Drain thoroughly. If desired, cut the noodles into thirds for easier handling.

3. Wash the bok choy and green onions and drain. Separate the bok choy stalks and leaves. Shred the leaves and cut the stalks into slices about 1 inch thick. Chop the green onions and ginger. Smash and peel the garlic. Rinse the canned bamboo shoots and water chestnuts in warm running water; drain thoroughly.

4. Heat the broth on the stove and bring to a boil. Add the vegetables and bring to a boil again. Transfer enough broth to fill the fondue pot about ⅔ full. Set the fondue pot on the burner, with enough heat to keep the broth simmering throughout the meal. (Keep the remaining broth warm on the stove to use as needed.)

5. Ladle a small portion of the broth with vegetables into the soup bowls. Invite guests to use chopsticks or dipping forks to cook the chicken in the hot pot. Dip the cooked chicken in dipping sauces, or enjoy with the bowls of broth. Use a dipping basket to remove the vegetables.

6. When the meat and vegetables are gone, add the noodles to the broth. Ladle out a bowl for each guest

Fondue Tandoori Chicken

Ingredients

- 2 tablespoons ground car-damom

- 4 skinless, boneless chicken breasts (about 7 ounces each)

- 2 teaspoons ground coriander

- 1 teaspoon ground cumin

- 2 teaspoons lemon juice

- 2 teaspoons ground cinnamon

- 5 cups oil, or as needed

- ¼ cup plain yogurt

- 2 cups Marvelous Mango Chutney

- ¼ cup sour cream

Directions

1. Blend together the ground cardamom, ground coriander, ground cumin, and ground cinnamon. Combine the yogurt and sour cream. Add 2 teaspoons of the spice mixture to the yogurt and sour cream. Store the remainder of the spice mixture in a sealed container to use another time.

2. Rinse the chicken breasts and pat dry. Use a knife to make cuts in the chicken. Rub 4 teaspoons of the yogurt and sour cream all over the chicken (use more than 4 teaspoons if necessary). Refrigerate and marinate the chicken overnight.

3. Stir the lemon juice into the remainder of the yogurt and sour cream. Cover and refrigerate until needed.

4. Cut the chicken into bite-sized cubes. Add the oil to the fondue pot, making sure it is not more than half full. Heat the pot on a stove element over medium-high heat.

5. When the oil is hot, move the fondue pot to the table and set up the burner. Skewer the chicken cubes so that the skewer goes right through the meat. Cook the chicken cubes in the hot oil for 2 to 3 minutes, until they are browned and cooked through. Serve with the yogurt and sour cream for dipping. Eat with the chutney.

Thai Coconut Chicken Soup

Ingredients

- 4 skinless, boneless chicken breasts (about 7 ounces each)

- 1 jalapeño pepper

- 1 tomato

- 10 fresh small mushrooms

- ¼ cup unsweetened coconut milk

- 2 tablespoons olive oil

- 2 teaspoons fish sauce

- 2 cups coconut milk

- 1 teaspoon lime juice

- 2 cups Homemade Chicken Broth

- 2 teaspoons brown sugar

- 2 garlic cloves, peeled

- 2 slices ginger

- 2 teaspoons turmeric

- 1 teaspoon lime juice

- ½ small yellow onion

Directions

1. Rinse the chicken and pat dry. Use a knife to make cuts in the surface. Combine the ¼ cup coconut milk, fish sauce, 1 teaspoon lime juice, brown sugar, whole garlic cloves, and turmeric. Place the chicken in a shallow glass dish and pour the marinade over. Refrigerate and marinate the chicken for at least 2 hours.

2. Preheat the oven to 350°F. Cut the marinated chicken into thin strips. Bake the chicken for 30 minutes or until cooked through.

3. Peel and chop the onion. Cut the chili pepper in half lengthwise and remove the seeds. Cut the tomato into wedges. Wipe the mushrooms clean with a damp cloth and slice.

4. Heat the olive oil in a saucepan over medium-low heat. Add the chopped onion and jalapeño pepper. Simmer on low heat for 5 minutes. Do not let the onion or pepper burn.

5. Add the 2 cups of coconut milk and the broth. Bring to a boil. Add the tomato, ginger, and mushrooms (or reserve the mushrooms to use as dippers, so that they soak up less of the spicy broth). Stir in the lime juice. Bring back to a boil. Transfer the broth to the fondue pot. Set the fondue pot on the burner, with enough heat to keep the broth simmering throughout the meal. (Keep the remaining broth warm on the stove to use as needed.) Dip the chicken

into the broth and warm briefly. Ladle out the vegetables in the soup.

Bacchus Chicken Fondue

Ingredients

- 1½ pounds skinless, boneless chicken breasts

- 2 tablespoons olive oil

- 2 cups dry white wine

- ¼ yellow onion

- 2 cups chicken broth

- 12 fresh small mushrooms

- Béarnaise Sauce

- 1 red bell pepper

- Aioli

- 1 orange bell pepper

- French Pistou with Cheese

- 1 garlic clove

- 2 parsley sprigs

- 1 French baguette, sliced

- 2 green onions

Directions

1. Rinse the chicken breasts. Pat dry and cut into thin strips. Chop the yellow onion. Wipe the mushrooms with a damp cloth and remove the stems. Wash the bell peppers, dry, and cut into strips. Peel and crush the garlic clove. Chop the parsley. Cut the green onions into thirds.

2. Heat the olive oil in a medium saucepan. Add the onion and garlic. Sauté until the onion is tender.

3. Add the white wine and chicken broth. Bring to a boil. Add the parsley sprigs and green onion; turn down to a simmer. Transfer the wine mixture to the fondue pot and set on the burner. Keep the wine mixture barely simmering throughout the meal.

4. Skewer the chicken strips and cook in the wine mixture for 3 to 4 minutes, until the chicken is cooked through. Cook the mushrooms and peppers in the wine mixture. Serve with the Béarnaise Sauce and Aioli for dipping. Eat with the French Pistou and the sliced baguette. Add other garnishes, side dishes, and condiments as desired.

Chicken with Coconut Rice

Ingredients

- 4 skinless, boneless chicken breasts (about 7 ounces each)
- 2 tablespoons olive oil
- ½ small onion, peeled and chopped
- 3¼ cups coconut milk, divided
- 2 cups long-grain rice
- 2 teaspoons fish sauce
- 5 cups oil, or as needed
- 5 teaspoons lime juice, divided
- ½ cup freshly ground black pepper
- 4 teaspoons brown sugar, divided
- Thai Peanut Sauce
- 2 garlic cloves, crushed

Directions

1. Rinse the chicken and pat dry. Use a knife to make cuts in the surface. Place the chicken in a shallow glass dish. Combine ¼ cup coconut milk, fish sauce, 1 teaspoon lime juice, 2 teaspoons brown sugar, and the crushed garlic. Pour the marinade over the chicken. Refrigerate the chicken and marinate overnight. Remove any excess marinade. Cut the chicken into bite-sized cubes.

2. Heat the olive oil in a frying pan over low heat. Add the chopped onion and cook until soft. Add the rice and sauté for 5 minutes until it turns shiny and is heated through.

3. Combine 3 cups coconut milk with 4 teaspoons lime juice and 2 teaspoons brown sugar. Add to the rice. Bring the rice to a boil, uncovered, on medium heat. Cover, turn down the heat,

and boil until cooked through, stirring occasionally. Keep the rice warm over low heat.

4. Add the oil to the fondue pot, making sure it is not more than half full. Heat the pot on a stove element over medium-high heat.

5. When the oil is hot, move the fondue pot to the table and set up the burner. Skewer the chicken cubes so that the skewer goes right through the meat. Cook the chicken cubes in the hot oil for 2 to 3 minutes, until they are browned and cooked through. Serve with the freshly ground black pepper and peanut sauce for dipping. Eat with the coconut rice.

Poached Chicken in Wine with Sweet Herbs

Ingredients

*   1½ pounds skinless, boneless chicken breasts

*   Béarnaise Sauce (Quick and Easy Blender

*   3 portions Sweet Herb Mix

*   Hollandaise Sauce

*   5 cups dry white wine, or as needed

Directions

1. Rinse the chicken breasts. Pat dry and cut into thin strips. Refrigerate until needed.

2. Add the Sweet Herb Mix to the wine and leave for 2 hours.

3. Strain the wine through a sieve to remove the herbs. Heat the wine on the stove in a saucepan or directly in the fondue pot. Transfer to the fondue pot if necessary, making sure not to fill the pot more than ⅔ full. Keep the wine simmering throughout the meal.

4. Use a dipping fork or metal skewer with a wooden handle to thread the chicken strips. Cook in the wine for 3 to 4 minutes, until the chicken is cooked through. Serve with the Béarnaise Sauce and Quick and Easy Blender Hollandaise Sauce for dipping. Add other garnishes, side dishes, and condiments as desired.

Chicken and Spinach with Tarragon

Ingredients

*   1½ pounds skinless, boneless chicken breasts

- 2 cups chicken broth

- 12 black peppercorns

- 1 tablespoon fresh tarragon, chopped

- 1 teaspoon ground cloves

- 1 teaspoon celery salt

- Quick and Easy Blender Hollandaise Sauce

- 2 pounds fresh spinach

- 2 garlic cloves

- 6 tablespoons olive oil, divided

- 1 cup Parmesan cheese, shredded

- 2 shallots, peeled and chopped

- 2 cups dry white wine

Directions

1. Rinse the chicken breasts. Pat dry and cut into thin strips. Refrigerate until needed. Stir the fresh tarragon into the Quick and Easy Blender Hollandaise Sauce and refrigerate until needed.

2. Heat 2 tablespoons olive oil in a medium saucepan. Add the shallots and sauté until tender. Add the wine and chicken broth to the sautéed shallots. Add the black peppercorns, ground cloves, and celery salt. Bring to a boil. Strain the liquid through a fine-mesh sieve.

3. Wash the spinach leaves, dry thoroughly, and coarsely chop. Peel and crush the garlic. Heat the remaining 4 tablespoons olive oil in a frying pan. Add the crushed garlic and cook for about 1 minute. Add the spinach and sauté briefly, tossing the leaves. Serve the spinach on a plate surrounded by the shredded Parmesan cheese.

4. Reheat the strained wine mixture on the stove either in a saucepan or directly in the fondue pot. Transfer to the fondue pot if necessary, move to the table, and set on the burner. Keep the liquid simmering throughout the meal.

5. Use a dipping fork or metal skewer with a wooden handle to thread the chicken strips. Cook in the wine mixture for 3 to 4 minutes, until the chicken is cooked through. Serve with the

Quick and Easy Blender Hollandaise Sauce for dipping. Eat with the spinach and cheese. Add other garnishes, side dishes, and condiments as desired.

Coq au Vin Fondue

Ingredients

- 1½ pounds skinless, boneless chicken breasts
- 1½ tablespoons olive oil
- 4 cups Burgundy wine, or as needed
- 2 carrots
- 10 fresh small mushrooms
- Light Horseradish Dressing
- 2 shallots
- 1 garlic clove
- Quick Honey Mustard
- 2 bay leaves
- Sour Cream and Mustard Dip
- 2 sprigs thyme
- 2 sprigs parsley
-

1. Rinse the chicken breasts. Pat dry and cut into thin strips. Peel the carrots; blanch briefly in boiling water. Drain thoroughly and thinly slice. Wipe the mushrooms with a damp cloth and slice. Peel and chop the shallots. Peel and slice the garlic clove.

2. Gather together the bay leaves, thyme, and parsley in a piece of cheesecloth about 6 inches by 6 inches. Use a piece of string to tie the cheesecloth and attach a cork to the other end of the string. (This makes it easier to remove the herb bouquet from the fondue.)

3. Heat the olive oil in a medium saucepan. Add the shallots and sauté until tender. Add the garlic. Add the Burgundy to the sautéed shallots. Lower in the spice bag. Bring to a boil. Remove the spice bag and transfer the liquid to the fondue pot. Keep the liquid simmering throughout the meal.

4. Use a dipping fork or metal skewer with a wooden handle to thread the chicken strips. Cook in the wine until the chicken is cooked through. Skewer the mushrooms and carrots and cook as desired. Serve with the sauces for dipping.

Ham, Cheddar, and Walnut Fondue

Ingredients

- 1 pound Cheddar cheese
- 1 teaspoon lemon juice
- 1½ tablespoons cornstarch
- 1 cup ham, chopped
- 1 garlic clove
- 2 tablespoons walnuts, chopped
- 1 French baguette, cut into cubes
- 2 tablespoons butter or margarine
- 2 tablespoons onion, chopped
- ½ cup sour cream

Directions

1. Finely dice the Cheddar cheese. Toss with the cornstarch and set aside. Smash the garlic, peel, and cut in half.

2. Rub the garlic around the inside of a medium saucepan. Discard. Melt the butter and add the chopped onion. Cook briefly, and stir in the sour cream.

3. Stir in the lemon juice. Add the cheese, a handful at a time. Stir the cheese continually in a sideways figure eight pattern. Wait until the cheese is completely melted before adding more. Don't allow the fondue mixture to boil.

4. After half the cheese has melted, stir in ½ cup of the cooked ham. When the cheese is completely melted, stir in the remainder of the ham. Add the walnuts.

5. Transfer to a fondue pot and set on the burner. Serve with the baguette cubes for dipping.

Deep-Fried Wieners

Ingredients

- 12 wieners

- 4 cups oil, or as needed

- ¼ cup cornstarch

- Basic Batter

Directions

1. Dust the wieners lightly with cornstarch. Place a skewer or stick through each wiener and place on a serving tray at the table.

2. Add the oil to the fondue pot, making sure it is not more than half full. Heat the pot on a stove element over medium-high heat. When the oil is hot, move the fondue pot to the table and set up the burner.

3. Invite guests to coat the wieners in the batter and cook in the hot oil until the batter turns golden brown. Drain on paper towels if desired.

Hearty Sausage Fondue

Ingredients

- 10–12 pork sausages

- Horseradish with Sour Cream

- 4 cups oil, or as needed

- Horseradish Cream

Directions

1. Thaw the sausages if necessary and pat dry. Cut into 2-inch pieces. Add the oil to the fondue pot, making sure it is not more than half full. Heat the pot on a stove element over medium-high heat. When the oil is hot, move the fondue pot to the table and set up the burner.

2. Use dipping forks to spear the sausages. Cook in the hot oil, turning occasionally, until they are browned and cooked through. Drain on paper towels if desired. Serve with the dipping sauces.

Two Pot Sausage Fondue

Ingredients

- 8 Italian sausages
- 2 tablespoons flour
- ¾ pound Gorgonzola cheese
- 1 tablespoon cornstarch
- ¾ pound mozzarella cheese
- 2 tablespoons cream
- 1 garlic clove
- 1 teaspoon nutmeg
- 1¼ cups milk
- 4 cups oil, or as needed
- 2 tablespoons butter

Directions

1. Thaw the sausages if necessary and pat dry. Cut into bite-sized pieces and set aside. Finely dice the Gorgonzola and mozzarella cheeses. Smash the garlic, peel, and cut in half.

2. Warm the milk in a small saucepan. In a separate medium saucepan, rub the garlic around the inside and then discard the garlic. Melt the butter in the saucepan with the garlic and stir in the flour. Add 1 cup of the warmed milk. Cook over low heat for about 10 minutes, whisking to form a creamy sauce.

3. Add the cheese to the milk mixture, a handful at a time. Stir the cheese continually in a sideways figure eight pattern. Wait until the cheese is completely melted before adding more. Don't allow the fondue mixture to boil. Add the remaining ¼ cup of milk as needed.

4. When the cheese is melted, dissolve the cornstarch in the cream and add to the fondue, stirring. Turn up the heat until it is just bubbling and starting to thicken. Stir in the nutmeg. Transfer to a fondue pot and set on the burner.

5. Add the oil to a second fondue pot designed for oil cooking, making sure it is not more than half full. Heat the pot on a stove element over medium-high heat.

6. When the oil is hot, move the fondue pot to the table and set up the burner. Use dipping forks to spear the sausage pieces and dip into the hot oil. Cook until browned. Dip the sausages

into the cheese fondue.

Tandoori Pork

Ingredients

- 1 large yellow onion

- 1 zucchini

- ½ teaspoon paprika

- 5 cups oil, or as needed

- 1 cup milk

- Tempura Batter

- ½ cup cornstarch

- 2 cups soy sauce

- 1½ pounds pork tenderloin

- 1 ⅓ cups plain yogurt

- ⅔ cup Instant Tandoori Rub

Directions

1. Peel the onion and cut into rings. Toss with the paprika. Soak in the milk for at least 1 hour, making sure all the onion pieces are covered. Drain the onion pieces and dust with the cornstarch.

2. Rub the pork with the Instant Tandoori Rub and cut into cubes. Cut the zucchini into pieces at least ½ inch thick.

3. Add the oil to the fondue pot, making sure it is not more than half full. Heat the pot on a stove element over medium-high heat. When the oil is hot, move the fondue pot to the table and set up the burner. Keep the heat high.

4. Coat the onion rings with the batter and drop the battered onion rings into the oil. Use a dipping basket if necessary. Cook briefly, turning occasionally, until they turn golden brown. Remove and drain on paper towels.

5. Use dipping forks to spear the seasoned pork and the zucchini and cook in the hot oil. Make sure the pork is cooked through. Provide each guest with a small bowl filled with ½ cup soy

sauce, and another bowl filled with $\frac{1}{3}$ cup yogurt, for dipping.

Pork "Satay" Fondue

Ingredients

- 12 large shrimp

- 1 tablespoon plus 1 teaspoon red curry paste

- 2 teaspoons salt

- 1½ pounds pork tenderloin

- 3 teaspoons brown sugar

- 2 garlic cloves

- 5 cups oil, or as needed

- 1 cup coconut milk

- Thai Peanut Sauce

- 2 tablespoons plus 2 teaspoons lime juice

Directions

1. Peel and devein the shrimp. Dissolve the salt in a bowl filled with 3 cups of warm water. Soak the shrimp in the water for 5 minutes. Drain. Cut the pork into cubes approximately 1 inch thick.

2. Smash, peel, and mince the garlic cloves. Combine the garlic with the coconut milk and lime juice. Stir in the red curry paste and brown sugar.

3. Lay out the pork in a shallow glass dish. Pour just over half of the coconut-milk marinade over the pork cubes. Refrigerate and marinate the pork for 1 hour. Mix the remaining marinade with the shrimp and marinate for 15 minutes. Remove any excess marinade from the pork and shrimp.

4. Add the oil to the fondue pot, making sure it is not more than half full. Heat the pot on a stove element over medium-high heat. When the oil is hot, move the fondue pot to the table and set up the burner. Keep the heat high.

5. Use dipping forks to spear the pork and shrimp. Cook in the hot oil — the shrimp will cook

more quickly than the pork will. Serve with the peanut sauce for dipping.

Bacon and Water Chestnut Appetizer

Ingredients

- 24 whole water chestnuts, fresh or canned

- 4 cups oil for deep-frying, or as needed

- 12 slices bacon

- 1 cup white sugar

Directions

1. If using fresh water chestnuts, peel, rinse, and drain. If using canned water chestnuts, rinse with warm running water and drain thoroughly.

2. Cut the bacon slices in half. Wrap each piece of bacon around a water chestnut, and use a toothpick to secure. Place the water chestnuts on a serving tray.

3. Add the oil to the fondue pot, making sure it is not more than half full. Heat the pot on a stove element over medium-high heat. When the oil is hot, move the fondue pot to the table and set up the burner.

4. Use dipping forks to spear the water chestnuts and cook briefly in the hot oil. Dip the cooked water chestnuts and bacon in the sugar.

Pork Balls in Coconut and Lime

Ingredients

- 12 ounces ground pork

- 3 pineapple chunks, finely minced

- ¼ cup coconut flakes

- 6 teaspoons lime juice

- 2 cups coconut milk

- 2 teaspoons fish sauce

- ½ cup light cream

Directions

1. In a medium bowl, combine the ground pork with the coconut flakes, lime juice, fish sauce, and minced pineapple. Mix together thoroughly.

2. Use your hands to form the ground pork mixture into 10–12 balls the size of golf balls.

3. Place the coconut milk in the fondue pot and bring to a boil. Turn down to a simmer and add the cream. Place the fondue pot on the table and set up the burner. Keep the liquid simmering while cooking the pork balls.

4. Use dipping forks to skewer the pork balls. Cook in the fondue until the pork is cooked through (about 5 to 7 minutes).

Sweet and Sour Pork Fondue

Ingredients

- 1½ pounds pork tenderloin
- 1 cup pineapple juice
- Sweet and Sour Marinade
- ½ cup red wine vinegar
- 6 tablespoons sugar
- ¼ pound baby carrots
- 6 tablespoons tomato paste
- 2 red bell peppers
- 5 cups oil, or as needed
- 2 green bell peppers
- ¾ cup firmly packed brown sugar
- 2 cups pineapple chunks, canned or fresh

Directions

1. Cut the pork into bite-sized cubes. Toss with the marinade. Place in a shallow glass dish, refrigerate, and marinate for 1 hour.

2. Blanch the carrots and bell peppers briefly in boiling water. Drain thoroughly. Cut the peppers in half, remove the seeds, and cut into bite-sized cubes. Cut the baby carrots in half.

If using canned pineapple chunks, drain and dry thoroughly.

3. Warm the pineapple juice and red wine vinegar in a small saucepan on low heat. Add the sugar, stirring to dissolve. Add the tomato paste and bring to a boil, stirring to make a smooth sauce. Add the baby carrots to the sauce. Keep warm on low heat. (The peppers can be added to the sauce or cooked in the oil.)

4. Add the oil to the fondue pot, making sure it is not more than half full. Heat the pot on a stove element over medium-high heat. When the oil is hot, move the fondue pot to the table and set up the burner. Keep the heat high.

5. Use dipping forks to spear and cook the pork cubes until lightly browned. Spear the pineapple slices and cook until lightly browned. Drain on paper towels if desired. Dip the pork into the sweet and sour sauce and the pineapple chunks into the brown sugar.

Sausages in Broth

Ingredients

- 9 ounces cooked summer sausage

- 2 tablespoons olive oil

- 5 cups Vegetable Broth (), or as needed

- 9 ounces cooked knockwurst

- 9 ounces cooked bratwurst

- Lemony Horseradish

- 1 pound asparagus spears

- Horseradish Cream

- ½ small yellow onion

Directions

1. Cut the summer sausage in half and cut each half into 3 wedges. Cut the knockwurst and bratwurst into pieces about 2 inches thick. Blanch the asparagus briefly in boiling water, and drain thoroughly. Cut the asparagus into 2-inch pieces. Peel and chop the onion.

2. Heat the olive oil in a medium saucepan on low heat. Add the chopped onion and sauté until the onion is soft and translucent.

3. Add the broth to the cooked onion and bring to a boil. Transfer enough broth to fill the fondue pot about ⅔ full. Set the fondue pot on the burner, with enough heat to keep the broth simmering throughout the meal. (Keep the remaining broth warm on the stove to use as needed.)

4. Use dipping forks to spear the sausages and asparagus and cook in the hot broth. Serve with the horseradish sauces for dipping. Ladle out the cooked onion and serve with the sausages.

Ham Roll-Ups

Ingredients

- 8 ounces cream cheese

- ¼ teaspoon black pepper

- 1 green onion, diced

- 4 cups oil, or as needed

- 1 teaspoon Worcestershire sauce

- Quick and Easy Batter

- 8 ounces cooked ham, sliced

- Quick Honey Mustard

- 2 eggs

- 1 tablespoon milk

Directions

1. Combine the cream cheese with the diced green onion and Worcestershire sauce. Mix together thoroughly and refrigerate until needed.

2. Cut each slice of ham into strips approximately 1 inch thick. Roll up the slices. If necessary, secure with a toothpick.

3. Beat the eggs with the milk and black pepper. Make sure the egg is beaten thoroughly.

4. Add the oil to the fondue pot, making sure it is not more than half full. Heat the pot on a stove element over medium-high heat. When the oil is hot, move the fondue pot to the table and set up the burner. Keep the heat high.

5. Use dipping forks to spear the rolled-up ham slices, removing the toothpicks if using. Dip

into the egg wash, and then coat with the batter. Cook the rolled-up ham in the hot oil until the batter is browned. Serve with the honey mustard and cream cheese mixture for dipping.

Cocktail Wieners

Ingredients

- 24 cocktail wieners

- 4 cups chicken broth

- 2 teaspoons orange mar-malade, optional

- Seafood Cocktail Sauce

- Sweet and Sour Sauce with Tomato Paste

Directions

1. Cut each cocktail wiener in half and set aside.

2. Add the orange marmalade to the Sweet and Sour Sauce with Tomato Paste. Keep warm over low heat.

3. Heat the broth on the stove and bring to a boil. Transfer enough broth to fill the fondue pot about ⅔ full. Set the fondue pot on the burner, with enough heat to keep the broth simmering throughout the meal. (Keep the remaining broth warm on the stove to use as needed.)

4. Use dipping forks to spear the cocktail wieners and cook in the hot broth. Serve with the sauces for dipping.

Lamb Kebabs with Sun-Dried Tomatoes

Ingredients

- 2 cups oil-packed sun-dried tomatoes

- 1½ cups Yogurt and Dill Dressing

- 1¾ pounds lean lamb

- Bruschetta with Roma Tomatoes

- ¼ cup fresh mint leaves

- 4 cups olive oil, or as needed

Directions

1. Drain the tomatoes and chop. Cut the lamb into bite-sized cubes. Place the lamb on a serving platter surrounded by the mint leaves.

2. Add the oil to the fondue pot, making sure it is not more than half full. Heat the pot on a stove element over medium-high heat. When the oil is hot, move the fondue pot to the table and set up the burner. Keep the heat high.

3. Use dipping forks to spear the lamb cubes. Cook in the hot oil until browned. Serve with the Yogurt and Dill Dressing for dipping. Eat with the bruschetta and the sun-dried tomatoes.

Indian Curried Lamb

Ingredients

- 2 tablespoons cardamom seeds
- 1 teaspoon turmeric
- 2 teaspoons ground coriander
- 1½ pounds lean lamb
- 4 teaspoons ground cumin, divided
- 4 potatoes
- 1 red bell pepper
- 2 teaspoons ground cinnamon
- 1 green bell pepper
- 1¼ cups plain yogurt, divided
- 1 tomato
- ¼ cup sour cream
- 1 tablespoon lemon juice
- 3 teaspoons curry powder
- 5 cups oil, or as needed
- 1 teaspoon freshly cracked black pepper

Directions

1. Crush the cardamom seeds with a mortar and pestle. Blend together the cardamom, ground

coriander, 1 teaspoon ground cumin, and ground cinnamon. Combine ¼ cup of the yogurt with the sour cream. Add 2 teaspoons of the spice mixture to the yogurt and sour cream. Store the remainder of the spice mixture in a sealed container to use another time. Refrigerate the yogurt dressing until needed.

2. Blend together the curry powder, 3 teaspoons ground cumin, black pepper, and turmeric. Rub into the lamb. Cut the lamb into bite-sized cubes. Boil the potatoes on medium-low heat for about 15 minutes, until they can be pierced with a fork but are not too soft.

3. Wash the red and green peppers, remove the seeds, and cut into cubes. Wash and chop the tomato. Stir the lemon juice into the remaining 1 cup of yogurt. Combine the yogurt with the peppers and chopped tomato and refrigerate until ready to serve.

4. Add the oil to the fondue pot, making sure it is not more than half full. Heat the pot on a stove element over medium-high heat. When the oil is hot, move the fondue pot to the table and set up the burner. Keep the heat high.

5. Use dipping forks to spear the lamb cubes. Cook in the hot oil until browned. Serve with the spiced yogurt mixture for dipping. Eat with the boiled potatoes and the pepper, tomato, and yogurt salad.

Lemony Ginger Cod

Ingredients

- 1½ pounds fresh or frozen cod fillets
- 4 cups oil, or as needed Parsley for garnish
- ¾ cup Lemony Ginger Marinade

Directions

1. Rinse the cod, pat dry, and cut into cubes at least 1 inch thick. Marinate for 30 minutes in the Lemony Ginger Marinade.

2. Add the oil to the fondue pot, making sure it is not more than half full. Heat the pot on a stove element over medium-high heat. When the oil is hot, move the fondue pot to the table and set up the burner.

3. Spear the fish cubes with a dipping fork and cook in the hot oil until browned. Garnish with

parsley. Serve with lemon juice or homemade dipping sauces as desired.

Fish Bathed in Broth

- 20 medium shrimp

- Fish Broth

- 2 teaspoons salt

- Quick and Easy Tartar Sauce

- 1 pound fish fillets (such as cod, sole, or flounder)

Directions

1. Peel and devein the shrimp, leaving the tail on. Fill a bowl with 3 cups of warm water, add the salt, and stir until it dissolves. Add the shrimp and leave in the warm water for 10 minutes. Rinse in cold water, drain, and pat dry with paper towels. Cut the fish fillets into bite-sized pieces.

2. Heat the broth on the stove and bring to a boil. Bring to the table and set up the burner. Be sure to keep the broth at a boil throughout the meal. Use a dipping fork to spear the shrimp and fish. Cook the fish and shrimp in the hot broth. Serve with the tartar sauce for dipping.

Bacon-Wrapped Shrimp

Ingredients

- 18 large raw tiger shrimp, peeled and deveined, tails on

- 4 cups oil, or as needed

- ¼ cup lemon juice

- 6 slices raw bacon

- ¼ cup sugar

- ⅓ cup fresh baby dill

Directions

1. Rinse the shrimp in cold water, drain thoroughly, and pat dry.

2. Remove any excess fat off the bacon and cut each piece into thirds. Take about ¼ teaspoon of the baby dill and place on the shrimp. Wrap a piece of bacon around the shrimp 2 to 3

times. Continue with the remainder of the shrimp. Place on a serving platter on the table.

3. Add the oil to the fondue pot, making sure it is not more than half full. Heat the pot on a stove element over medium-high heat. When the oil is hot, move the fondue pot to the table and set up the burner.

4. Use dipping forks to spear the shrimp. Cook in the hot oil for about 30 seconds. Serve with the remaining dill, lemon juice, and sugar for dipping.

Mediterranean Salmon with Pesto

Ingredients

- 1½ pounds fresh salmon steaks

- Cilantro and Mint Dressing

- 4 cups olive oil, or as needed

- 1 jar capers

- Italian Pesto with Basil and Pine Nuts

Directions

1. Rinse the salmon, pat dry, and cut into cubes at least 1 inch thick.

2. Add the oil to the fondue pot, making sure it is not more than half full. Heat the pot on a stove element over medium-high heat. When the oil is hot, move the fondue pot to the table and set up the burner.

3. Spear the salmon cubes with a dipping fork and cook briefly until browned all over. Serve with the pesto and dressing for dippers, and the capers as a garnish.

Shrimp with Peppercorn Dip

Ingredients

- 24 large raw shrimp

- 4 cups oil, or as needed

- 2 tablespoons black peppercorns

- ¼ cup freshly squeezed lemon juice

- 2 tablespoons white peppercorns

Directions

1. Peel the shrimp, including the tails, and devein. Rinse the shrimp in cold water, drain thoroughly, and pat dry.

2. Use a pepper grinder to grind the black and white peppercorns. Combine in a small serving bowl. Place the shrimp on a large serving platter.

3. Add the oil to the fondue pot, making sure it is not more than half full. Heat the pot on a stove element over medium-high heat. When the oil is hot, move the fondue pot to the table and set up the burner.

4. Use dipping forks to spear the shrimp and cook in the hot oil until they change color. Serve with the peppercorn mix and lemon juice for dipping.

Teriyaki Marinated Salmon

Ingredients

- ¾ cup Quick and Easy Teriyaki Marinade

- 1 cup baby carrots

- 8 ounces sugar snap peas

- Yogurt and Dill Dressing

- 8 ounces fresh small mush-rooms

- Speedy Garlic Mayonnaise

- 4 cups oil, or as needed

- 1½ pounds fresh salmon steaks

Directions

1. Prepare the marinade, the yogurt dressing, and the mayonnaise at least 1 hour ahead of time. Refrigerate the dressing and mayonnaise until ready to serve.

2. Rinse the salmon, pat dry, and cut into cubes at least 1 inch thick. Marinate the salmon for 1 hour.

3. Wash the vegetables and drain thoroughly. Blanch the peas briefly in boiling water and then plunge into ice water and drain thoroughly. Cut the mushrooms into 2 to 3 slices, but don't slice too thinly.

4. Add the oil to the fondue pot, making sure it is not more than half full. Heat the pot on a

stove element over medium-high heat. When the oil is hot, move the fondue pot to the table and set up the burner.

5. Spear the salmon pieces with a dipping fork and cook briefly in the hot oil, turning occasionally, until browned all over (less than 1 minute). Cook the mushrooms and carrots briefly. Dip the carrots and sugar snap peas into the yogurt dressing or the mayonnaise. The teriyaki salmon and mushrooms can be dipped or enjoyed as is.

Angels on Horseback

Ingredients

- 36 canned Pacific oysters

- 1 cup bread crumbs

- 12 slices raw bacon

- 4½ cups oil, or as needed

- 6 eggs

Directions

1. Dry the canned oysters thoroughly. Cut any excess fat off the bacon and cut each piece into thirds. Wrap a piece of bacon around each oyster and secure with a toothpick.

2. Place each egg in a small bowl and beat lightly. Place the bacon-wrapped oysters on a serving plate and give each guest a bowl with a beaten egg. Place the bread crumbs in a bowl beside the oysters.

3. Add the oil to the fondue pot, making sure it is not more than half full. Heat the pot on a stove element over medium-high heat. When the oil is hot, move the fondue pot to the table and set up the burner.

4. Use dipping forks to spear the oysters. Invite guests to dip the oyster into the beaten egg and then into the bread-crumb coating. Cook the oysters until the bread crumbs turn a golden brown (about 1 minute).

Easy Seafood in Broth Dinner

Ingredients

- 2 cups frozen broccoli and cauliflower

- 10 frozen fish sticks

- 4 cups chicken broth

- 20 frozen breaded shrimp

Directions

1. Thaw the frozen broccoli and cauliflower and pat dry. Place the frozen seafood and vegetables on a large platter.

2. Heat the chicken broth in a fondue pot over a stove element. Bring to a boil, then move the fondue pot to the table and set up the burner. Keep the broth simmering throughout the meal. Use a dipping fork to spear the fish and vegetables and cook in the hot broth.

Tempura Shrimp

Ingredients

- ¾ pound (15–20) large shrimp

- Tempura Batter

- ¼ cup flour

- 4 cups oil, or as needed

- 1 lemon

Directions

1. Peel and devein the shrimp, leaving the tail on. Rinse the shrimp in cold water and pat dry with paper towels.

2. Lightly dust the shrimp with the flour and set on a serving plate. Cut the lemon into wedges. Garnish the shrimp with the lemon wedges. Place the batter in a separate bowl.

3. Add the oil to the fondue pot, making sure it is not more than half full. Heat the pot on a stove element over medium-high heat. When the oil is hot, move the fondue pot to the table and set up the burner. Use dipping forks to spear the shrimp and dip into the batter. Cook in the hot oil until golden brown. Drain on paper towels if desired.

Caribbean Butterflied Shrimp

Ingredients

- 12 large raw shrimp, peeled and deveined, tails on

- ½ cup light cream

- 4 teaspoons lime juice

- 2 garlic cloves

- ½ cup rum

- 1 firm banana

- ¼ teaspoon curry powder

- 1 tablespoon butter or margarine

- 1 cup sweetened coconut flakes

Directions

1. Rinse the shrimp in cold water and pat dry with paper towels. To butterfly the shrimp, make an incision lengthwise down the back. Cut down as deeply as possible without cutting right through the shrimp. Halfway down the back, make two parallel cuts on the left and right of the incision. Flatten down the 4 quarters as much as possible. Place the butterflied shrimp on a large serving platter.

2. Smash and peel the garlic. Peel the banana and cut into slices at least ½ inch thick.

3. In a medium saucepan, melt the butter on low heat. Add the garlic and cook on low heat in the melting butter for 2 to 3 minutes. Add the cream and the lime juice. Carefully add the rum. Stir in the curry powder.

4. Transfer the dish to a fondue pot and set on the burner at thetable. Use dipping forks to spear the shrimp and cook in the fondue until they change color. Dip into the coconut flakes. When the shrimp are gone, add the banana to the fondue and dip into the coconut flakes.

Shabu-Shabu for Two

Ingredients

- ½ pound sirloin beef

- 2 cups cooked rice

- ½ cup canned bamboo shoots

- Instant Dashi

- 1 small carrot

- ½ cup Lemon-Soy Dressing

- ½ head Napa cabbage

- 2 eggs

Directions

1. Cut the meat into paper-thin slices. Rinse the bamboo shoots in warm running water and drain thoroughly. Wash the carrot, peel, and dice. Wash the cabbage leaves and rip into chunks.

2. Place the beef and vegetables on a platter in separate sections. Place each egg in a small bowl and beat. Place the rice in a separate serving bowl.

3. Heat the dashi broth on the stove and bring to a boil. Transfer to the fondue pot. Set the fondue pot on the burner, with enough heat to keep the broth simmering throughout the meal.

4. Cook the meat and carrot in the broth. Dip the cooked food into the dipping sauce and/or the beaten egg. Serve the rice with the food. When the beef and carrot are gone, add the bamboo shoots and cabbage to the broth, cook briefly, and then eat the soup.

Printed in Great Britain
by Amazon